OUT of the Devil's Cauldron

A Journey From Darkness to Light

Santeria
Spiritualism
Palo Mayombe

John Ramirez

Heaven & Earth *media*

a division of John Ramirez Ministries

Contents

Acknowledgments

I am a bondservant of Jesus Christ, and therefore with deep appreciation I wish to express a sincere thanks to those who encouraged me to write down my testimony and make it a book.

First and foremost, I would like to thank my Lord Jesus Christ to whom I give all the glory, all the honor, and all the praise! Without Him this book would never have become a reality.

To my pastor, David Wilkerson, from Times Square Church, I thank Jesus Christ for the many times I had the pleasure of walking you home and the many words of wisdom you shared with me on those nights. They really impacted my life. I have been touched twice in my life—once by Christ and the other by you. As I walked you home one night after service, I left you in front of your home. You could have said many things to me, but you said, "I see Jesus in you." Thank you, Pastor, for those words that encouraged me all the more to tell the world what God has done in my life.

For my home church, Times Square Church in New York City, where the seasoned preaching and teaching of the Word of God in my time of need sustained me. A heartfelt thanks to Pastor Carter Conlon, senior pastor at TSC. Thank you, Pastor Carter, for sharing your favorite Bible scripture with me. It blessed me deeply, and I made it my own as well: Psalm 112. You said you were going to have it engraved in a mirror and put it up in your home. Awesome idea!

To Pastors Alexander and Sandra Sarraga from Champions Ministries in Orlando, Florida. In life, the Lord blesses us with many relationships. But I never knew the Lord would be so good as to bless me with two people as special as you. Your discipleship and mentoring has been instrumental in God's plan for my life. I thank the Lord for both of you. You are a big part of my life.

To Pastor Sandra, thank you for your editing skills and creative thinking. I also want to thank Pastor Alexander for his graphic design gift. Thank you for the beautiful book cover. Your God-inspired gift made it what it needed to be.

I also want to thank God for my beautiful daughter, Amanda. I thank God every day that of all the daughters in the world, He gave me you. I'm blessed to have you as my daughter.

To my mother, whom I love with all my heart. I thank God for you every day. You have not only been a great mother but you have also taken the role of a dad in my life. Thank you for all the great things and the great examples that you put into my life.

To my sister in the Lord, Angie Kiesling, who I thank God for with all my heart. I thank Him for divinely putting us together for such a time as this and for allowing you to edit the testimony of my life. When I needed an editor, and had so many to choose from, I'm blessed that the Lord chose you. Not only are you an outstanding and excellent editor, but you are also my personal friend.

To my dear friends Jose Ponce and Julio Nieves for being true brothers in the Lord. I love you dearly, and I thank God for both of you and for always sustaining me in prayer. And to Peter Torres, whom I love for being a true brother in the Lord. I thank God for the many times we met at the altar in the mornings for prayer and also the many times we ministered together.

To my sister in Christ, Olga Rodriquez, for taking on the challenge of typing up my testimony of what God has done in my life.

I want to thank all the people at churches, radio stations, TV stations, colleges, and high schools who supported my ministry in allowing me to share my testimony.

To each reader who has purchased this book. I thank God for the privilege of allowing His miracle in my life to change yours.

Prologue

I was a devout follower of Santeria, *espiritismo*, and Palo Mayombe, a Palero high priest *tata* and warlock. We called it "the religion." For twenty-five long years, I had no idea I was enslaved to an unspeakable evil, deceived into believing I was God's servant and lost in a hideous cult that taught its members to hate and kill, all under the guise of worshipping God. Then one day the Holy Spirit revealed the great lie that had kept me blindfolded for years. Yet with no strength or will of my own to break free from the religion (those who tried were threatened and suffered a penalty of death), I continued doing what I did, admiring cult members who said they loved God. But one day the miraculous happened. I was set free just like the apostle Paul.

> *As he journeyed, he came near Damascus, and suddenly a light shone around him from heaven. Then he fell to the ground and heard a voice saying to him, "Saul, Saul. Why are you persecuting me?" And he said, "Who are you, Lord?" Then the Lord said, "I am Jesus, whom you are persecuting. It is hard for you to kick against the goads." So he, trembling and astonished, said, "Lord, what do you want me to do?"* Acts 9:3-6

With that, I made a clean getaway through the cross of Jesus Christ. That was how I was delivered from the one who was dragging me to an eternal hell—Satan himself. This is my testimony.

Mark of the Beast

S hifting my feet to fight the cold, I waited at the busy crosswalk and watched my breath disperse like smoke in the wintry air. Though the temperature hovered in the low-20s, the main street through Castle Hill in the Bronx teemed with people as it always did this time of day. A cluster of little kids played at the curb, seemingly unaware of the traffic roaring past them just a few yards away. Someone leaned on their car horn and shouted obscenities at another driver. A police car zigzagged through traffic, its siren blaring and bleeping to make a path through the crush of vehicles. *Home sweet home,* I thought cynically. The light changed.

"Hey, John! What's happenin'?" a voice shouted.

I looked up to see a man I recognized from Step-In, the corner bar near the train station, leaning against the door of the barbershop. "Not much, man. Just keepin' it cool," I replied. We slapped hands in passing before I quickly turned the corner down a side street, not wanting to make small talk.

The cold wind whipping through Castle Hill hit me full in the face, and I turned up the collar of my wool coat. Though the winter chill invigorated me physically, something nagged at my mind—a troubled feeling I couldn't shake. I glanced up to see an older Hispanic woman outside her storefront staring at me, and as I turned my dark, piercing eyes on her, fear swept over her countenance. She made the sign of the cross and hurried inside, a bell jingling in her wake.

Go to your aunt's house. The same thought I'd had earlier that day came again, this time more insistent. By now it was unmistakable: the spirits were speaking to me. *Go to your aunt's house.* I considered not going, but only for a minute. Changing directions, I looped back the way I'd come but avoided the main street, arriving at Aunt Maria's three-story clapboard house within minutes. I rang the doorbell and waited, then rang it again. After the third ring I decided she must not be home, but something told me to go knock on the basement door. Stepping through the chain-link gate that accessed the basement entry, I started to knock when I saw that the door was already cracked open. I walked in.

Eerie vibes filled the room—vibes I knew well—and instantly I realized some sort of witchcraft ritual was in process. Through the dark I saw my aunt, a man, and another woman sitting at a *mesa blanca*, a "white table" used for witchcraft readings. I glanced at the floor in front of the table and saw strange symbols written in chalk with lighted candles on them, making it appear as if the floor were on fire. For the first time I got a good look at the man sitting behind the table. Short and stocky, he wore a bandana around his head like a biker, and his medium-length black hair was matched by coal-black eyes that seemed to pierce right through me. Whoever he was, I could tell he was in charge of this gathering, and his mysterious aura was strangely beckoning.

My aunt waved me over, not wanting to interrupt the reading. As the reading went on, I stared at the symbols on the floor, fascinated by the power and heaviness that hung like a lead cloak over the room. Witchcraft was no stranger to me—I had been casting spells and growing to new levels of power since I was ten years old—but the energy coming off this man was like nothing I'd ever felt before. Whatever it was, I wanted it too.

I listened as he described the different aspects of this religion until finally my curiosity won out.

"Hey, what's going on?" I whispered to Aunt Maria.

"This is Palo Mayombe," she replied in a monotone, tucking a strand of her salt-and-pepper hair back under her white bandana. As she said that, the man turned to me and opened his mouth to speak. My heart thumped like a jackhammer in my chest when I heard the words of his prophecy.

"This young man is your right hand and most faithful person in the occult," he said to my aunt. He held my eyes for a long moment, letting the words sink in. "He is a very powerful warlock who will become a major player in the religion. He must be in the first group of new initiates next month because of his power and commitment to Palo Mayombe."

Aunt Maria's eyes widened with awe, and I watched as a slow smile spread across her face. In that instant we both knew I had just walked into a supernatural appointment—her nephew was about to become a major power player, controlling spiritual regions of the Bronx.

That afternoon was a turning point for me. I knew I was going to another level in the spirit realm and would have power like I never knew before.

Contract with the Devil

The priesthood ceremony took place two weeks later in the basement of Aunt Maria's house. As I approached the house on foot, I could feel the rhythm of the conga drums vibrating on the night air. The sound of chanting inside told me that those who came to watch the ceremony—seasoned priests of the religion—were beckoning the spirits, setting the spiritual atmosphere for what would take place on that night in February 1997.

Opening the basement door ushered me into a world few people will ever experience. My aunt's basement had been transformed into a ritualistic chamber, dressed for a serious witchcraft ceremony. Flickering candles cast mysterious shadows on the walls, and seventeen tree branches covered the floor, one for each of the initiates to sit on. Two or three dozen roosters squawked from a makeshift cage in the corner of the room. I knew what they were for.

The music got louder and the songs more intense, with lyrics inviting the devil to come as the hours ticked toward midnight. Somebody asked the helpers to bring us into another part of the basement, and we stood shoulder to shoulder in front of what I sensed to be an altar. I felt the presence of demons so thick I could almost touch it. When the drumbeats reached their fullest a heavy presence beyond human comprehension descended on the room. Even though the words chanted were African and

Spanish, I knew in my heart and soul and spirit they were summoning the devil.

It was *Nafumbe*, the devil himself.

Beads of sweat broke out on my forehead, and a strange mix of terror and excitement swelled within me. At five minutes to midnight, the high *tata* priest stood in front of me and started chanting some words, spelling out the contract that was about to take place. He chose me to go first. Taking a one-edged razor, he cut into my flesh. As my blood ran, I knew the contract was being initiated.

Out of the seventeen initiates that night, the devil chose only me to be initiated as *tata*, the calling of a high priest. The godfather cut a pentagram into the flesh of my right arm, distinguishing me from the others. The priests boasted about how seldom one is singled out for the calling of *tata*, and I held my head high: I had the mark of the beast on my body.

Early the next morning I woke up, bloody and swollen from the night's ritual, and made my way to the bathroom. It was still dark out and very quiet, but I could tell from the single small window in the basement that dawn would come soon. I flipped the switch to turn on the light and leaned in close to peer at my reflection in the mirror.

The face that stared back at me was the face of a new person, a new man. The black eyes that gazed from the reflection were eyes I had never seen before: I had been born into Palo Mayombe to be a *Palero tata*—a high priest.

Chapter 1

Beginnings

My blood boiling with rage, I walked into a bar and scanned the smoky room for my father, knowing he had to be here. Where else would he be when he was not at home or driving his gypsy cab? And there he was, just as I expected—sitting on a barstool, leaning in close to a woman with dark hair in a tight blouse. He was smiling and laughing, and I knew thoughts of my mother were far from his mind.

A movement across the room caught my eye. A man I'd never seen before glared at my father and clenched his fists. Even from this distance I could feel a thick vibe of jealousy and anger radiating from him.

The strange man reached inside his coat, and in that moment I realized what he was about to do—what I had secretly wanted somebody to do for a long time: kill my father.

Two shots rang out, and as my father slumped to the wooden floor, the stranger crossed the room to pump the rest of the bullets in the barrel into his cold, vile heart. While my dad lay dying, the bullet holes still smoking, I stepped from behind the stranger and stared down at my father's face. His eyes grew wide, and as his soul's silver cord was snapping I told him all he needed to do was show some love and concern for his wife and family. Just a little. Then his firstborn son would not have spent so many days and nights of his young life wishing his father was dead and finally seeing it come true.

The last words he heard me say were: "I wish it had been me who pulled the trigger instead."

* * * * * * * * * * * * * *

The wail of a siren jarred me from sleep, and I sat bolt upright in bed, shaking in a cold sweat. *A dream... it was only a dream.* The same one I'd had over and over again since my father's murder the year I turned thirteen. I looked over at my brothers, snoring softly through the uproar of the South Bronx streets outside our dingy apartment window. The room was freezing as usual, but I was used to it. Unable to sleep, I crossed to the window and peered out. A couple of neighborhood thugs huddled over a trashcan fire on the corner, and a second police car roared down the street, its sirens chasing after the first one that had awakened me from the cruel dream.

How did I get here? I wondered. I was born in Puerto Rico but grew up in the Bronx as the oldest of four sons. From the Caribbean island of Puerto Rico, with its glorious sunshine, palm trees, warm breezes, and crystal waters, we moved to the harsh, cold streets of the South Bronx. As a child, I would fold my arms on an open windowsill on one of the upper floors of our apartment building and look out at the trash-cluttered sea of concrete, glass, and brick buildings. I had an artistic soul, even as a boy, but for miles into the horizon I saw no art or beauty. All I saw was an ocean of ugliness.

Goodhearted by nature, I was a spirited child who did my best to help my mother and brothers out. I knew my mother loved me, and that was very important, but what I craved most was my father's approval and love. It was something every growing boy needed. I longed for a dad to participate in my life, to say he was proud of me and that he loved me. It was something I never got.

Instead my absentee father had countless women on the side, bar fights, and drunken rages. His insane exploits ensnared him and saddened us deeply. I felt seething resentment even at a young age that he cheated us of a normal family's prosperity, blessings, and happiness.

His careless, cruel behavior toward my mother and our family became more horrible with each passing year. I would go from being a kind boy to being a very angry one. As time went on, my feelings and outlook on the world festered with the bitterness I felt. Eventually my once-kind heart turned stone cold.

The Bittersweet Big Apple

My mother, Esther Martinez, was only a sweet sixteen-year-old when she married Eustaquio Ramirez in Santurce, Puerto Rico, and gave birth to me that same year in December 1963. The very next year she gave birth to my brother Julio. We stayed in Rio Piedras, Puerto Rico, for one year until my parents and both sides of their families came to the United States.

Upon arriving in America, in rapid succession my brothers George and Eustaquio Jr. came along. But the challenges grew deeper. As I got older I realized our family had not been prepared for the realities of living in New York.

This was supposed to be the start of a better life in the most promising city in the world—New York. Manhattan was the island that was so close, yet from where we lived in the South Bronx, it seemed a world away. It often felt like we were trapped in a time warp. We lived in an apartment prison with invisible bars that caged us in an endless, living nightmare.

The reality in which we lived seemed like a bad dream. My father, who was supposed to take the lead, instead was constantly running out of the home and out of our lives. He was missing in action for most of our lives. But when he did park the gypsy cab he drove for a living, we'd hear his keys jingle in the lock and he'd swing the front door open to step back into our lives. "*Papi's* home!" one of my younger brothers would yell. My dad was a young and handsome man with piercing eyes and thick black hair. Within seconds, bustling in her housedress and ever-present apron, my mother would put away any anger because of his absence, and her heart would be taken in again just by the sight of him.

He'd stroll into the kitchen for a bite to eat as though he had never left.

"What's the matter with these sons of mine?" he complained to my mom, pointing his finger at us as we stood in the doorway between the tiny living room and the cramped kitchen.

"They're good boys, Eustaquio. What do you mean?" my mother said, stirring a pot of yellow rice on the stove.

"If they were *good boys* they would ask for my blessing whenever they see me on the street like their cousins do," my father said. "*'Bendicion, Tio!'* they always say, but do my own sons ever ask me to bless them? No— all they ever want is a dollar so they can go buy candy." He glared in my direction, assuming that as the oldest I spoke for all four of us boys. Bitterness and hatred churned in my heart. I knew that a reply of any kind was useless. And then my father would make his way to the living room, fall out on the sofa in a drunken stupor, and go to sleep.

Often the next morning, although we were his own family, he seemed so detached, like his mind was elsewhere. It was as if he needed to be treated more like visiting royalty than a father, and we all tiptoed around and tried our best to please him and make him part of our lives.

My mother probably wanted to tell him news of her last few days or weeks. My brothers and I were bursting to share our baseball victories or basketball stories or talk about what happened in or after school. Maybe mention some cool car we saw or some girl we had a crush on, or even share a funny joke we heard. But more often than not we just ate in relative silence, afraid to say much of anything.

There seemed to be a gateless fence with barbed wire around him that we were afraid to scale, knowing we'd get cut. At other times it seemed more like a brick wall that we could never break through where he kept his emotions walled in, never expressing any real joy or love for us.

I never knew who my father really was and won- dered if he even liked us, but I couldn't figure out why not. I saw other boys with their fathers going to the park, hitting a ball, playing catch, talking about sports. Those fathers would talk enthusiastically with them, pat them on the back, and walk along with their sons, sharing a good laugh. I yearned for that kind of relationship, but no matter what I tried he'd just push me away and call me "stupid." Some words are shattering to a child, and *stupid* is certainly one of them.

My father didn't seem to care that his dysfunction was so damaging. He seemed to go out of his way to discourage my brothers and me, to criticize us and talk to us in a condescending tone. We were never good enough to make him happy. And I swore I'd never be like him when I became a father and a man. I hated who he was, and I was even ashamed to tell others he was my dad.

Every now and then I held out hope that he would look at me and it would spark a glimmer of affection—in that moment he'd remember the little boy he once was. Or he'd want me to look up to him as the man I would one day become, but he left no positive impressions. The picture was either distorted or ugly or strangely blank. He left no template for me to pour myself into, no image for me to model myself after.

He frequently made promises, and like fools we let our hopes get high.

"Hey, John," he would call from the sofa, a beer in his hand. "This weekend, once my shift is over, I'll take you and your brothers to Coney Island. What do you say to that, huh?" His smile looked so genuine I believed him. "Want to go to the amusement park? Obey your mother all week and we'll go do the rides on Saturday."

But Saturday would come and my father was nowhere to be found. He had run out of our lives once again, to be missing for days or weeks on end.

Mom was the backbone of the family. With four children at a very young age, it was difficult for her to do things and move around from place to place. Since my mother was poorly educated and had no work experience outside the home, we depended on public assistance, food stamps, and whatever help my mother could get. Everything ran out after only a week or two, but we tried to make the best of it. From time to time my father would give her twenty dollars to buy food for the week. Even back then, that was not enough.

But at times it was much worse than that. Once I walked into the kitchen and stopped cold, staring in amazement at the five dollars he had left on the counter for food and other necessities. *Five dollars!* For his wife and family of four growing boys! Even with my grade school math I knew that five people (six whenever he came back home), divided by five dollars, meant my dad had left less than a dollar apiece for each of us to live on for the week. I also knew that even in the late '60s and early '70s that was no money. My mother used the basics—rice, beans, and potatoes—to stretch everything. But even with her creative and good cooking, five dollars was just a bad joke. What my father had left for us to survive on was more of an insult than a help.

"Five dollars! You know that's not enough to feed a family," my mother pleaded, her brow creased with worry lines.

"Then maybe you should put the five dollars in some water and stretch it," my father called back over his shoulder, a sneer on his face as he laughed at his joke. That was one of the many ways he humiliated my mother and controlled the family, by leaving us in lack.

Where Are You, God?

Like so many others, my father was involved in *espiritismo* (spiritualism) and appealed to his gods in a darkened room with strange rituals, chanting, and candles. To him it was just a cultural thing. One afternoon toward dusk I walked down the hall of our apartment and heard my father chanting in the bedroom he shared with my mother. Tiptoeing to the door, I peeked through the crack and saw him before a makeshift altar glowing with candles. The sight of my father chanting to his favorite saint, whom he called *San Lazaro* (St. Lazarus), both frightened and fascinated me.

He often sent me with five dollars to the nearby *botanica*, a potion store, to buy an orange candle and flowers for *San Lazaro*, whom he probably loved more than his own kids. I could still hear his words throbbing in my mind: "Hurry and don't lose the money!" I would run down the stairs like a bat out of hell, trying to catch my breath and running past the people sitting on the front stoop. I was on a mission, dashing through cars in heavy traffic, my hands tightly gripped on the money. As I ran into the *botanica*, I hoped and prayed they would have what my dad sent me to buy. If they didn't, he would be disappointed—and angry with me.

Unlike many other Hispanic families, my family never went to the big Catholic church in our neighborhood, but I had seen the crucifixes and pictures of Jesus and heard people call Him "God." If He was God, why didn't He show up in my life? Why did He allow my brothers and me to hurt at the hands of our own father—not to mention the anguish my mother endured? I pushed the thoughts aside as quickly as they came. It was too painful to dwell on what the answer might be.

One afternoon I went down the block to play in the schoolyard, but to my surprise I heard loud music emanating from it. Curious to see what all the commotion was about, I drew nearer and saw a large red tent with a church service going on underneath. Somebody was playing a keyboard, and a choir swayed at the back of the tent as they belted out songs about Jesus. For a while I stood at a distance, touched by the music and stirred up in my heart. I couldn't put my finger on it, but instinctively I knew something very special was going on in this place. While the choir sang, a man came around off the stage and touched people on the forehead randomly. Whenever he touched them, they fell to the ground onto their backs, as if going to sleep. They looked so peaceful lying there, and suddenly I wanted the same thing to happen to me. I felt a love there that was indescribable.

As if on cue, the man leading the event started moving in my direction. My pulse quickened. One by one he touched people in the crowd near me, the closest one being a man standing right next to me. The man fell out on his back, and I could see the blessing on him—that something special I longed for too. I looked up expectantly, waiting for the minister to touch me, but he had passed me by, moving to another section of the crowd instead. I left that event feeling heartbroken, unwanted, and unloved. Why couldn't it be me they prayed for? Why couldn't it be me they touched? The answer that flickered through my mind: *I guess God doesn't love me either.*

My Father, My Enemy

Most nights my father came home already roaring drunk and enflamed by rage. For no reason at all, or any feeble excuse, he would beat my mother. My brothers and I cowered in our rooms, trembling with fear. We were all just little boys, and I would bite my lip and beg God to make the screaming and hitting stop.

One night the sound of my mother screaming pulled me out of a deep sleep. I leaped from the top bunk bed where I slept and stumbled down the hallway, my stomach churning in knots. As I approached the kitchen, the sound of shattering glass exploded in the air. My dad had come home drunk—at two o'clock in the morning—and demanded the meal my mother always had waiting for him.

"You good-for-nothing woman! I don't know why I put up with you!" he yelled, looking for something else to throw. My mother sobbed as she tried to serve him the dinner she spent all afternoon cooking. Suddenly a reheated meal of beans, rice, tomatoes, chicken, and plantains went airborne as he slammed his dinner plate against the wall.

"*Eustaquio, no-o-o!*" my mother wailed. I watched my father's face—her reaction flipped a switch in his drunken brain and unleashed a monster.

He grabbed her by the hair and began to beat her mercilessly. At one point during his pounding, my mother—literally knocked out of her shoes by him—managed to break away and run barefoot in terror down the hall into their bedroom. She struggled to lock the door in a futile effort to escape him. He lunged after her and broke down the door, and her screams grew louder as the beating continued. Though I was still a young boy, I knew I had to rescue her. I bolted into the room and jumped on my dad's back to stop him from hurting my mother. He turned around, eyes blazing with fire, cursed me, and tore me off him with rough hands, throwing me violently across the room. I hit the floor hard in a broken heap, feeling physically and emotionally hurt, angry, and power-less as he continued to beat my mother.

Finally, at four o'clock in the morning, his rage spent, my father passed out and the house returned to its now-eerie quiet. Shaking with fear and anger, I crawled back into my bunk bed and tried to go to sleep. In just three hours I would have to wake up, get dressed, and go to school as if nothing had happened. I would have to show a brave face to the world, pretending that my home life was not the living hell it truly was.

That night as I examined my bruises and thought about the injuries my mother must have too, my hatred for my father grew stronger. It was that night I first wished my father was dead. I didn't realize it then, but one day my wish would come true.

Chapter 2

The Burnt-Out Bronx

Instead of getting better, life stumbled on with violent scenes repeating themselves as if on a demented loop, spiraling further and further down in our circular, hellish way of life. As my father's neglect grew worse, our family's financial condition sank to frightening new lows and we moved from place to place in the Bronx. In those days, slumlords wouldn't repair their buildings, and the notorious slum villages lined the garbage-strewn streets of the South Bronx. No one who lived in the other boroughs was rushing to visit anyone in the Bronx back then. It was like a ravaged war zone.

Dishonest landlords set their own buildings ablaze for the insurance money, and the area became known as "the Burnt-out Bronx." The nighttime sky would glow orange with fire whenever a slumlord decided to cash in his investment. In one apartment building, thirty families filled the dingy, cramped living spaces, but because the building was so rundown, many families moved out, leaving only three families—including ours.

This building had no hot water or heat in the winter, and some nights my brothers and I slept in our clothes, bundled in our sweaters, coats, scarves, and gloves just to stay warm throughout the night. We huddled in our rooms, the air so cold it felt almost like camping outdoors, with icy blasts of air coming from our mouths as we tried to get some sleep.

Shamed by the squalor, we nonetheless clung to the apartment because we had nowhere else to go, and my brothers and I took shifts staying up late watching out the window to make sure the local hoodlums didn't burn the building down, thinking it was abandoned.

I stood by the window, my eyes heavy with sleep but forcing them to stay open as I watched outside, alert for any movement or the sound of breaking glass, signaling the approach of neighborhood "bandits" on the prowl looking for fun. I glanced over at the clock—the faint glow of the hour hand ticked off the hours…one o'clock, two o'clock …until my shift ended at 3 a.m. I stared out the window at the cold night, the light from the corner streetlamp shining into our bedroom window. Though my body yearned for sleep, I stood guard making sure my family wasn't burned to the ground.

Gangs ruled the different neighborhoods of the Bronx, and ours was no different. A gang called the New York Reapers patrolled the streets and alleyways we called home, and in a strange paternalistic way they took care of the neighborhood residents—saving their blood-thirst for any rival gang members foolish enough to try to come onto their turf.

And when the rival gangs *were* foolish enough to encroach on Reaper turf, it was time for a rumble.

"Hey kid," a Reaper called to me, tapping his car horn to get my attention. His pimped-out Chevy Nova idled at the curb, the exhaust pipes rumbling. I glanced up from my task of filling two buckets with water from the fire hydrant. Once full, my brother Julio and I would stagger up five flights to our apartment, which had no running water, and return to make the same trip six or seven more times until there was enough water for the evening. I pretended not to hear him...maybe he would go away.

"Yo, *kid,* I said, you listening to me?" There was no way I could ignore him now. I looked him straight in the eyes, a flat expression on my face.

"A rumble's going down tonight with the Flying Dutchmen, so get your chores done and make sure your family's inside by eleven o'clock. You hear me? We don't want nobody gettin' hurt—except the Dutchmen." He cackled at his joke and slid his hand along his slick black ponytail, a flash of silver showing from the thick, studded rings he wore on his fingers—the better for fighting with.

I nodded and went back to my chore, but I could feel my heart pump faster. Rumbles were frightening, no doubt about it. But they were also exciting. As soon as the Nova roared around the corner, I shouted to Julio.

"Julio, there's a rumble tonight! Tell Mom, George, and Eustaquio!" My little brother was just emerging from our building with two empty buckets in his hand, ready for the next refill and trip back up the five flights to our apartment.

His eyes widened. "Really? What time?"

"Eleven o'clock. C'mon, go tell Mom so she can run to the market. I'll get this round." Taking the empty buckets from my brother, I watched as he shot like a cannonball back toward the front stoop of our building and disappeared inside.

A weird, almost tangible vibe ran up and down the streets of the neighborhood. Like an electric current, news of the rumble spread. Mothers did last-minute shopping at the battered storefront shops along Deli Avenue and 179th Street. Little kids playing by the street jittered in a crazy hop-skip dance, and horns blared from cars, as if signaling the coming showdown between the rival gangs.

And at eleven o'clock, we would be ready for them. My brothers and I leaned on our open bedroom window-sill like we had ringside seats to a championship prize fight. "George, Julio—make sure Eustaquio doesn't lean out too far!" I commanded protectively, assuming the role of little father figure in the absence of our real dad. In every direction we could see, people hung out their windows like we did. The only thing missing was the popcorn and Coke. A murmur of voices zigzagged across the streets and alleyways, now strangely empty except for the rats that scurried along behind the line of overstuffed garbage cans.

As if on cue, the Reapers took up their posts along the streets, inside alleyways, and up on the rooftops of the buildings, toting bats, chains, knives, machetes, guns, and trashcans full of bricks. As the Flying Dutchmen rolled into our neighborhood, a war whoop sounded from the rooftops, where they rained bricks down onto the rival gang members' cars while the Reapers on the street level dragged them out of the vehicles and beat them mercilessly. The Reapers came out like savage animals, and suddenly the streets below us churned with bodies and blood and the screams of broken men.

Confined to a one-block radius, the rumble roared on, and my brothers and I watched fascinated from five stories high. Close to five hundred gang members tore up the street below, jumping all over the cars, thrashing rival members, and firing gunshots into the night. Others were laid out in the street—the ones who might not make it home tonight or live to see another day. Not a cop was in sight. The police both feared and respected the gangs and had a sixth sense about when a rumble was going down. After an hour or so of brutality—their bloodlust spent for the night—the victorious Reapers celebrated, standing on the street corners drinking beer and whooping. But the act of vengeance wasn't complete until they stripped the "colors" off the Flying Dutchmen and hung the rival gang members' denim jackets from every lamppost in the neighborhood, declaring the Reapers' victory.

An eerie quiet returned to the neighborhood, the only sound coming from the *flap-flap* of denim jackets hanging on the lampposts. My brothers and I crawled into bed and tried to sleep, our hearts pumping adrenaline—a natural internal protection against the cold on winter nights.

The Proving Ground

Violence has a trickle-down effect, and not just the gangs lived by the warrior code in the South Bronx. We kids did too. Even if you tried to avoid it, it found you. The tough kids—the thugs in the neighborhood—always tested news kids on the block, and since we moved around so much, my brothers and I constantly had to prove our mettle. These were the walking time bombs, the lowlifes in the neighborhood who wanted to get their way all the time, so they beat up on the weaker kids. If you didn't stand up to them, or take part in whatever they demanded, your lunch money would mysteriously disappear at school and you might not make it home without a black eye or broken fingers.

I stood up to them but tried to play it cool, not wanting to become a thug like them.

"Hey, John! Come 'ere," a voice called one day as I walked home from school alone. It was Jose, the leader of a group of lowlifes that hung around the basketball court whistling and jeering at the girls who walked by and making life miserable for any guy who wasn't a part of their group.

"I can't, I got to get to work," I lied, pretending that a job other than my usual water-hauling chores beckoned me.

"Now, you know we're not gonna let you off that easy," Jose said, sidling up to me with five of his cronies hanging back, ready for action judging by the look in their eyes.

I sized up the competition. Jose I could take, and maybe one or two more—but six against one were bad odds.

Jose felt my hesitation and smiled a slow, devious grin. "We're gonna go down to the store and get a snack… thought you could pick up a few things for us. What d'ya say, boys? Is John good enough to be one of us?" His friends sniggered and watched for my reaction.

I knew Jose wanted me to steal some candy bars, potato chips, and maybe a few canned drinks for them. Either I did it or I would be labeled a sucker.

Jose took his pocketknife out of his jacket and pretended to clean his fingernails, making sure I saw the shiny silver of the blade. "I'm not hearing an answer. Yo, are you down with us or are you a punk?" He looked up at me, his eyes glazed with hatred now. "'Cause if you're a punk we're gonna beat your face in." He flipped his knife in the air. "Maybe even cut you up a little."

"I'm not scared, I just don't wanna waste my time doing that," I said, looking Jose straight in the eye. The truth is I didn't want to get caught stealing and end up with a record like all these hoodlums did. I wanted to finish school, not go to jail with these lowlifes, but my thoughts were saying one thing and my mouth was saying another. "Sure, I can do that, man. I just don't want to. Why you tryin' to test me?"

Bartering for time never worked with guys like Jose. They kept after you till you did it. I never got caught—I stole ice cream from the ice box, potato chips from the rack, sodas from the refrigerator. On other days pricier items made the hit list, and we'd all walk into a store and steal a jacket or two. I gained Jose's respect but lost my own.

Shuffling home after a petty theft, I'd see my father's cab parked at the curb in front of a bar and watch as he opened the passenger side door for a pretty woman—his latest mistress or good-time girl. Sometimes he caught me staring at him and made a funny face in return, as if to say, *Hey, boys will be boys...don't tell your mom!*

Hatred churned in my gut, a hatred honed to a razor-edge by his years of neglect and abuse. If he were a protective father, a real dad, maybe I wouldn't have to stoop to stealing candy bars just to keep the neighborhood thugs at bay. Maybe our home life would be *normal*...that crazy word that always eluded the Ramirez family.

Walking on Eggshells

In spite of our miserable existence, my brothers and I looked up to our mother as our hero. She did the very best with everything, and she did whatever she could for us. But my father's drinking grew even worse, and he became more abusive and savage than I thought possible. Soon he began demanding things, taking valuables and money from us. Sometimes he grabbed the money my mom had spent months scraping together—nickels and dimes—to buy his liquor, and often he'd snatch back the meager money he had just left us for the week.

I walked around holding my breath as soon as he left, afraid to relax. Finally, no sooner had I let out a sigh of relief, no sooner had my mother, brothers, and I restored the craziness to order, harmony, and some small degree of peace, than my father would come back in and destroy everything again.

Things began to fall apart even more financially. We lived in the slum apartment buildings for what seemed like an eternity because it took my mother years to save up enough money for us to move out. Her worried face saddened my brothers and me; we knew she wanted the best for us but could not give it. But we were rich in the love she gave us. In spite of everything, we could count on just one thing—our mother loved us. Yet she seemed strangely bound to our tormentor, my father, and powerless to do anything about it.

Once in a while my dad bought things for us, and then months would pass before he bought anything substantial again. The end of the year and the holidays especially were a tough time in our home. When school started in September, it was the first strain of the end of the year on our meager household budget. My brothers and I had no choice but to wear the same clothes and coats from the year before because there was no money to buy new things.

"High waters!" some kid would yell as I got in line at the school cafeteria for lunch, mocking the way my pants rode a few inches above the tops of my shoes. "Hey, isn't that your little brother's coat," another might call out. "It looks kind of short in the arms." I played it off, trying to act as if I wasn't embarrassed by the jeers, but the words sank deep into my spirit, fueling my resentment against my father.

The Dark Side Calling

For my brothers and me, Halloween kicked off the annual holiday season. We loved the masquerade nature of it, getting to be a superhero, cowboy, Count Dracula, werewolf, or ghost for a night. It was fun going from house to house to collect bags of candy apples and fruit, chocolate bars, and candy corn. Some years all four of us were decked out in our Halloween glory, and other years only two of us got real costumes due to the slim household budget. For the two of us left out, my mom compensated by painting our faces, transforming us into ghouls and devils from the neck up.

"George, Julio, Eustaquio…come *on!*" I yelled impatiently from the front door of our apartment, my face painted red like the devil, makeshift horns on my head. I had just looked in the bathroom mirror one last time and grinned at my reflection—my eyes, painted black as coal, even freaked me out a little.

Mami came down the hall pulling Eustaquio by the hand. He kept tripping on his long black vampire costume and sounded muffled through the plastic mask that covered his face. "You keep an eye on your little brothers, you hear?" she said, pinning me with *the look*. "I want you boys back by 8:30 at the latest."

I promised her we would and off we went, taking the stairs two at a time to get outside as fast as possible. The streets of the Bronx came alive on this night, with costumed kids darting this way and that across the noisy streets. Even the hookers that worked the street corners traded their usual miniskirts and fishnet stockings for provocative Halloween costumes like cats and Playboy bunnies. We met up with some of our friends and headed for an apartment building rumored to have the best candy in the neighborhood.

"Oh, man, you gotta check out this one house!" my friend David said, his voice breathless from running in his Batman costume. "The lady who lives there made it into a haunted house with—"

"Don't spoil it!" I shot back. "Let me see for myself."

As we climbed the stairwell inside the building, I heard scary music playing and deep throaty voices chanting from the third floor. My heart beat faster, and when we hit the third-floor landing I saw that whoever lived there had transformed the entire area around her door into a witch's lair with cobwebs, black lights, dangling skeletons, and black cat figurines. The door to the apartment was open, and white smoke poured from the dark room beyond. Our creaking footsteps on the landing signaled whoever lived there, and she flew out at us dressed like a witch, screaming and cackling into the hallway. We shrieked and laughed, enjoying the good Halloween scare, then held our bags out for the candy she offered. I went back to her door four times that night.

My fascination with the dark, mysterious nature of the underworld gained a foothold that year, and the supernatural seemed to step out to meet me. I started seeing things that shouldn't have been there—or rather I saw things that *weren't* there…in the physical realm. Years later, as a warlock and high priest of Santeria, I would look back on this time of adolescence and realize my spiritual eyes were being unlocked for the very first time.

One night, after playing down the street with my friends, I came into our building and headed for the stairwell. Our apartment was located on the third floor, and as I rounded the corner at the first landing, a strange, dwarfish woman with a distorted cartoon-like head popped out from behind the second-story stairwell. She looked human, but her head was impossibly large—all I saw was this freakish head popping out, a clown smile on her face. My heart froze in my chest and I lunged back to the first floor. After waiting ten minutes, I tried again… and again…but every time I advanced up the stairs, she popped out, blocking my passage.

The woman looked very young, with long black hair and pale white skin. I had never seen anyone like her in our building before, and a sick feeling in my gut told me something was not right. *She* was not right. Desperate to get home, I ran back to the main lobby to see if anyone was going upstairs so I could walk up with them and make it past the dreaded second-story stairwell.

"Hey, can you help me, sir?" I called out when a man finally entered the lobby. He stopped and listened as

I described my predicament—and the strange dwarf lady on the second floor—but when he went to check things out, he called back down to me, "There's nothing here, kid! You're seeing things!" and made his own way up the flights of stairs.

It took me an hour to finally make it home; in the end I walked upstairs with another resident of the building, and of course the dwarf lady never showed up.

Another night, at my grandmother's house, I looked out the back window and saw a tall woman in a red dress running from one side of the alley to the other— except she didn't run, she floated. Back and forth she went, in quick succession, and as she glided by she would turn her head and smile as if taunting me. Terrified, I ran into the kitchen.

"*Abuela,* come quick! There's a lady outside," I said, tugging on my grandmother's arm.

She turned from the stove and looked at me. "What do you mean, Johnny? There are lots of ladies in this neighborhood." But something in my eyes spoke to her, and an instant later she followed me back to the living room.

"Shhh. We have to surprise her," I said as I hid behind the curtains and gestured for my grandmother to do the same. A worried look framed her face, and I knew she realized that whatever I had seen impacted me greatly.

I peeked around the edge of the curtain. "There!" I said in a loud whisper, but my grandmother was too late. By the time she glanced out, the gliding lady had floated out of sight, leaving only a flash of red behind. Once again, the apparition seemed intended for my eyes only, no one else's.

One day weeks later I ran outside to meet a friend in the vacant lot beside our apartment building, and we fell into a rock-throwing competition, seeing who could score the most hits at a window on the sixth-story building across the street. Tommy and I stood a good distance apart, taunting each other—"I got a better aim," "No, I do." Our verbal jabs volleyed back and forth, and suddenly something dropped from the sky and landed at my feet. I bent down to see what it was and saw a beaded Indian necklace with bright colors lying on the ground. I stuffed it in my pocket before Tommy could see because I knew he would try to take the necklace from me.

In that same instant I heard someone call my name, and it sounded like my mother. "My mom's calling me!" I yelled to Tommy as I ran toward home. But my mother never called me. Years later I realized what I heard was a familiar spirit—a principality that roamed the air. When I went into our building, I kissed the necklace and put it around my neck. *This is going to protect you* was the immediate thought that came to my mind. A few years later, when I took my first steps into witchcraft, my main spirit protector was an Indian chief that called itself Tawata. It was this spirit that threw the necklace out of the sky, I realized—initiating me to the dark side before I ever even heard the word Santeria.

Unbeknownst to me, the strange portal into the supernatural was opening wider, and in my youthful innocence and hunger for a father figure I walked right into it—without realizing the price I would pay.

A few months later I stayed over at my Aunt Lydia's house one night, and as the clock inched toward eleven she asked me to run to the store to get a gallon of milk for the morning. I put on my sneakers, stuffed the money deep in my pocket, and ran down the stairs to the street below. In the street, I started fast-walking across the avenue toward the convenience store five blocks away, ignoring the cluster of Reapers gathered here and there on the street corners.

After picking up the milk, I started back toward my aunt's apartment down the dark streets of the Bronx. Without warning I felt something creepy following me, and I cast backward glances over my shoulder. Looking up the street, from a distance I saw a blue Chevy parked under a streetlight. *That looks like my dad's car,* I thought to myself. The closer I got the more familiar the car looked. "That is *Papí's* car," I said out loud. As I approached the car I saw a man slumped over the steering wheel and knew it was him. Excited but nervous, I went up to the window and tapped.

"*Papí, Papí,* are you okay? Do you need my help?" I could tell he was very intoxicated, so much so that he couldn't drive and probably didn't even know where he was parked. He rolled down the window. For a fraction of a second my heart lifted and filled with compassion for him. Maybe this would be a father/son bonding moment—my chance to be a hero and rescue my dad for the night.

His voice came out in a pathetic slur, but I understood every word. "What are you doing, *stupid.* Leave me alone! Go home!" As I walked away I felt my heart shatter, and I knew that this person I called *Papí* was never my dad. I buried him that night in my thoughts, in my heart, in my life because he demolished me to the point where I wished he was dead. I came home a different boy that night. As far as I was concerned, I was open for a new love in my life, a fatherly love to a son. Where would I find it?

Chapter 3

Initiation

The year I turned ten my Aunt Maria, my father's sister, called my mother and convinced her to go to a tarot card reading. For some reason, my mom brought me along, perhaps as moral support for this venture into the unknown.

We turned down a side street near Tremont Avenue, stopping in front of a white two-story house situated close to the curb. A buzzing neon sign in the front window read "Tarot Card Readings."

Inside, beyond a small sitting area with a few chairs, I saw a curtain hanging over a door that led to a back room. *That must be where they do the readings,* I guessed, and sure enough within a few minutes the lady of the house came through the curtained doorway, gesturing for us to follow her back.

"This is my sister-in-law Esther and her son John," Aunt Maria told the woman, who eyed my mother and me for a few seconds, then nodded and told Aunt Maria to sit at the card table set up in the back room. A white cloth covered the card table, and I saw candlesticks, crosses, figurines of Catholic saints, and other "holy" items spread across another longer table against the back wall of the room.

Right away the woman, Cookie, gave Aunt Maria a card reading, and as she muttered out what she read in the cards, I glanced at my aunt's face. No one from our immediate family knew she had been involved in witchcraft since childhood—somehow she'd kept it a secret—but even now as I watched her, I saw a gleam in her eyes that hinted at a restrained power behind her bland exterior.

When Cookie finished she asked my mother if she would be interested. Mom hesitated, but Aunt Maria convinced her so my mother agreed, afraid to say no and disappoint her sister-in-law.

During my mother's reading, Cookie told her nothing but negative things. I couldn't believe the words coming out of her mouth.

"Your husband is a womanizer," she said, studying the cards on the table. "You have a very bad marriage, and I see you being a widow at a young age."

I glanced at *Mami*. Her face wore a blank expression, and I knew it was because the card reader's words had found their mark. She went on for a few minutes, loading my mother up with misery. The next thing she said was about me.

"Your son is on the verge of losing his sight…" She stopped suddenly, studied the cards a bit longer, and lifted her diabolical gaze toward me. *This boy needs a ceremonial cleansing right away. If he doesn't receive the cleansing I see him losing his eyesight within thirty days!* She turned her hard eyes back to my mother. "The ceremony will cost $200—don't delay."

By now my mother was in a panic. Beads of perspiration dotted her pretty forehead, and my stomach roiled with anger that one more thing just got added to her already heavy load of worries. She promised the card reader we would return within a week for my cleansing ceremony.

As we left the card reader's house that day, little did my mother know that an evil door had just been opened, and we were about to walk through it.

Welcome to Witchcraft

I knew my mom didn't have $200, and the idea of asking my father for the money was a joke, so she did what any good mother would do—she sold her bedroom set to a neighbor for $250.

A week later my mother took me back to the tarot card reader, who was a high priestess and medium in an occult religion called Santeria. Leaving my mother in the front sitting area, Cookie led me back to the kitchen where she initiated the cleansing ceremony by placing beads of different colors on the table, each strand representing one of the five main spirit gods that ruled the religion.

In the kitchen, I sat and talked with her until someone from behind me tied a blindfold around my eyes and led me to a room where together they tore off my clothes and bathed me with herbs and plants. Terrified, I shook with fear but kept silent. Why couldn't my mother be with me during this strange ritual that was both frightening and humiliating? I had no idea what would happen next.

Suddenly the high priestess and her helper started singing songs to the five main gods of Santeria: *Obatala, Yemaya, Ochun, Chango,* and *Oya.* Although I couldn't see because of the blindfold, I knew that two people performed this ceremony. Sometime later they dressed me in white and took me to another room where I was offered up to the five gods. When they finished singing, I was given five beaded necklaces to wear, each representing the color of a particular god. They told me to bow down in a certain fashion, repeat the names of the five main gods, and thank the gods for receiving me.

During the process the two women became my godmothers in Santeria. They wrapped my head in a white bandana and told me I must stay dressed in white for seven days. Finally they released me back to my mother, but I would never be the same innocent ten-year-old boy again. The world of Santeria had become real to me. My life would be controlled by the guardian spirits that rule over *espiritismo* and Santeria. I would no longer belong to my mother but to incredible forces beyond my control, for these entities had stepped up to fill the void in my heart that yearned for a father.

After this, every weekend one of my godmothers took me to what they called *centros* (*espiritismo* churches) to learn how to work the *mesa blanca.* I learned from the very best, people dedicated to Santeria and *espiritismo* for thirty, forty, fifty years of their lives. They called themselves mediums. As I made my weekly visits to the *centros,* I learned how to communicate with spiritual forces of different ranks, cast spells, and recruit others into the religion—spirits that I now realized were diabolical spirits, or demons.

School for Warlocks

Centro was a place where humanity met the supernatural in a most diabolical way, a place where I went to "school" to learn how to lend my body to evil spirits—to be demon-possessed. We met at Cookie's house in a large room on the first floor. About sixty people gathered in rows of folding chairs set up facing the *mesa blanca*. Aunt Maria took me there for the first time on a Friday night. As I walked inside the room, my eyes adjusting to the dim glow of candlelight, I felt chills run up and down my spine. Something in the atmosphere told me this was not a regular meeting. People stood in clusters talking before the service, but they took their seats when the six mediums assumed their place at the white table. Glancing around, I saw that I was easily the youngest one there, so I sat somewhere in the middle, trying to lose myself among the older people. But there was no chance I'd be lost that night.

"We have a special guest tonight," Cookie said as she called the service to order, dressed all in white. "He's a new initiate in the religion. John, would you come up here please?" She held out her hand toward me, a motherly expression on her face, and I couldn't refuse in front of all those staring adults. I walked to the front and Cookie sat me on the edge of the *mesa blanca* so I could watch, listen, and learn as the mediums worked the table.

No lights were allowed, because demon spirits only come down when it's dark, as Aunt Maria had told me before. The service started about 9 p.m. I had no idea that first time it would last until five o'clock in the morning. One by one the mediums performed cleansings, gave readings, and prophesied over those in the folding chairs who had come for healing or guidance or deliverance from spells.

"Focus and watch what we're doing," Cookie whispered to me. I nodded, instinctively aware that I should remain silent. "Permission of the white table," she suddenly intoned. "I see..."—and she called out what she saw in the large vase full of water in the center of the table, encircled by candles. The spirits showed her and the other mediums certain things in the water, or in their mind/conscience, and they would call those things out, addressing the person the prophecy pertained to. In time I grew bold enough to start speaking out things I saw in the water too, or the different vibes and spirit voices hovering over the table.

The mediums would target individuals in the audience, placing a glass of water and a candle behind their chair. "Permission of the white table, I see this lady who lives in your house—pale white skin, jet-black hair—and she's put a spell on your family. Now we're going to break that spell," one of the mediums said. The woman in the chair shook visibly, tears spilling down her cheeks. As the medium continued prophesying over the woman, he prepared himself to "catch" the demon that was casting the spell over the family, entrapping it in his body.

Suddenly the medium started yelling like a madman, foaming at the mouth. His eyes rolled back in his head, showing only the whites, and he practically floated in the air before grabbing the victim by the throat. The other five mediums around the table got up and started to pray—"Hail Mary, full of grace..."—throwing holy water on the medium in the chair. One medium grabbed a cross in her hand and confronted the demon trapped in the medium's body. Every time a spray of holy water hit the medium, his body jerked and contorted. By this point, I could see that the medium was in a trance—no longer himself but something diabolical. "Don't hit me! Leave me alone!" he screamed in the guttural voice of the trapped spirit. Finally, he fell back as if dead, growling and making weird noises as the other mediums drove the demon spirit back to hell.

"Permission of the white table," Cookie called out one night, directing her dark eyes toward me. "I see one of the most powerful guardian spirits in all *espiritismo* guiding and protecting you, John." Her words hung in the air as I waited for what would come next. "He is an Indian chief spirit named Tawata," she added, and at that moment I remembered the Indian necklace that had dropped out of the sky when I was younger. Amazed, after that I prayed to this special new deity—*my* protective spirit—daily, even moment by moment.

At another gathering one night, the intensity of the service reached an electrifying pitch, and I felt pulled to keep glancing at this six-year-old girl who'd been brought there by her mother. My sharpened spiritual senses picked up an evil vibe in the same instant the mediums at the white table shouted, "Focus, focus! There's a bad spirit in the air tonight, and the bad spirit is trying to grab some-body and take them with him." As they spoke, I felt the vibe of the spirit try to snatch the little girl. Before our astonished eyes, she hopped out of her seat, jumped up in the air, and spun around like a ballerina—spinning and spinning nonstop for several minutes. Her eyes were not her own, her hands were not her own, and her feet were not her own as they floated, not even touching the floor.

Later that evening at the white table, Aunt Maria stood paralyzed without blinking or moving her features for over an hour, looking like a mannequin. Dressed all in black for a change, she stood trapped in a trance with a demon that was new to the occult but not new to her. I left the service even more astonished about how the demon world worked, and I learned something new—not only how powerful the spirits of the dark side could be, but also that they have no respect for age. The purity of that six-year-old was snatched away that night. She was now one of us, never to be an innocent child again.

This was the life I lived for weeks on end, months on end, and years on end. After the service was over, often an adult would pull me aside and smile down at me. "You're going to be something great in this religion," one might say, a look of admiration in their eyes. "We can't wait to see how far you're going to go in Santeria," another would echo. "You're going to be very powerful. You will win many souls..."

Even though I didn't understand these predictions at the time, I felt like I was a part of something that wanted me for once. I was part of something great. For the first time in my life, I enjoyed the acceptance and love I never got from my father. I looked forward to the next validation the following Friday night.

Chapter 4

The Silent Pain

The school bell dismissing class rang out shrill and loud, cutting off the teacher's last words—"… your final grades, and have a happy holiday!"—but we kids didn't care. We were *free*…for two whole weeks. A couple of desks got overturned in the mad dash for the classroom door, and once we broke out into the halls they cleared within seconds amid loud whoops of celebration and ghetto-blasters cranked to ear-splitting levels. It was *Christmas*. Nothing could contain our excitement.

"Hey, John, I'm gettin' some good stuff this year. What about you?" my friend Junebug shouted as we pushed through the outside door into the freezing air of the schoolyard. Everybody turned to see what my response would be.

"My brother, I'm gonna get the bike I always wanted and my GI Joe set," I said boastfully, then turned around and murmured under my breath, *"Like I'm really gonna get these toys this year."* But Mom had said that this year my father was going to cooperate and be part of our Christmas—even promised it—so I allowed myself a spark of expectation. My brothers and I had a good feeling that, for the first time, we were going to have a good Christmas.

"Man, Christmas is my favorite holiday," Junebug went on. "Christmas at my house is always the best time of year—we always get the very best. My father always does the right thing."

"Really? Well, at my house we always step it up for the holidays," I lied, falling into the rhythm of things.

"Hey, you wanna go hang out? You wanna go to the candy store?"

"Nah, man, I gotta get home. My brothers and I are gonna help my mother put up the lights on the window and decorate the Christmas tree—my dad's supposed to bring home a tree today." We talked on as we headed down the block toward our apartment building, our feet crunching over clods of icy snow stained brown from the street sludge. People jostled along the streets with the ever-present noise of traffic and police sirens in the background. New snow started to fall as we walked, covering the dingy Bronx neighborhood in a fragile coat of white. In spite of myself, I really *did* feel hopeful about Christmas this year.

When I burst through the door of our apartment, there was the Christmas tree, still bound with twine and leaning in a corner of our tiny living room. *Mami* came in from the kitchen smiling. "Guess what we get to do tonight, John?" she said, her eyes sparkling.

"Did *Papi* bring the tree? It sure is a good one," I said, admiring the spindly balsam fir, my voice loud with excitement. "But Dad brought it, right? Just like he said he would?"

My mother's eyes flickered. "Of course he wanted to, but *Papí* was very busy with his taxi service today, so your Uncle Alberto brought it instead. It is a good tree, isn't it? We'll decorate it with lights and ornaments and make it real pretty for Christmas morning. Your father promised to be here this year—remember how I told you that? It's going to be a good Christmas, you'll see."

A twinge of disappointment bit at my insides, but I pushed it away, determined to be happy for my mother. Later that night we hauled the box of ornaments and lights down from the closet shelf. My brothers and I transformed that plain-looking tree into a real Christmas tree. In our childish glee we didn't notice how few ornaments and lights there really were. To us, it was the most beautiful Christmas tree we'd ever seen. I imagined waking up Christmas morning, running down the hall into the living room, and finding gifts piled underneath the branches, just like they did in the movies. After all, he had *promised* this year.

The days leading up to Christmas passed quickly, and suddenly it was Christmas Eve. After I helped clear the dishes away from the dinner table, I went over and stood beside my mom as she scraped leftovers into a container. "What time is Dad coming home tonight?" I gazed at her face and watched for her reaction.

She paused a second too long. "Oh, I'm not sure, but he'll be here for Christmas morning." She smiled at me and placed the container in the refrigerator. "He's bringing the gifts he promised. You and your brothers are gonna have your toys to play with in the morning."

"Okay," I said, mustering a feeble smile.

That night I leaned out the window of my bed-room and looked up at the stars, praying to the only god I'd ever known—the Indian spirit who gave me my protective necklace. "Tawata, please let my dad come home for Christmas like he said he would." I fingered the necklace around my throat and squeezed my eyes shut. "For once, let him show up."

Home for the Holidays

The grayish light of dawn peeked through the cracks around the window blind, signaling the start of a new day. My groggy mind took only half a second to register... *Christmas!* I kicked back the covers to awaken my brothers. We tore down the hallway and spilled into the living room.

"Santa came! He came, he came!" Julio shouted, jumping up and down and diving under the tree to look at the five gifts lying there. George and Eustaquio tumbled in after him. I didn't want to spoil the whole Santa thing for my younger brothers so I played along, my own heart thudding with excitement that *he* came—or rather came through. My father had come home for Christmas and brought presents for his family.

"Wait for your dad to come into the living room before you can get your toys," Mom said as she entered the room, tying on her robe.

"The toys are there. Grab your toys and don't make a mess," Dad's booming voice called from the living room doorway. "And make sure you clean up after yourself." He spoke with coldness and a pretend smile on his face.

"Merry Christmas, boys," Mom said as she bent down to kiss each of us on the cheek. "I'm gonna start breakfast."

My father settled himself on the couch and popped open a beer—breakfast in a can as one of the older boys in the neighborhood called it. He ordered my little brothers to hold off on the gifts until he passed each one of us the present with our name on it. I knew he wanted to do the father thing, and that was cool. It was good to see him home with us for once after so many Christmases when he was an absentee dad.

"Here you go, John." My father handed me a small gift wrapped in Christmas paper. It was too small to be a GI Joe, but I didn't care. I started to open the present and glanced up at Mom in the kitchen. She smiled back at me from the stove, where the smell of eggs frying wafted out into the living room.

My fingers struggled to tear open the gift, it was taped so much.

"Here, stupid, let me do it," my father said, snatching the gift out of my hands. "What kind of a kid can't even open his own Christmas present. Ay-yi-yi…" He made a hand gesture as if to slap me.

My heart, so full of joy at seeing my family all together on this special day, sank into the pit of my stomach. With his cruel, sarcastic comment, my father had killed whatever Christmas spirit resided in the Ramirez household.

I don't even remember what my present was that Christmas morning—some trinket my father picked up at Cheap Charlie's Store—but it didn't matter. In that one instant of cruelty he had spoiled it all.

A few days after Christmas, my father long gone from our lives again, I was heading down the apartment stairwell when I spotted two brand-new GI Joes lying on a step. One of the neighbor boys must have been playing with his new Christmas toys and got called inside for supper. I scooped up the action figures and tucked them under my shirt, then made a dash for my aunt's house where I could play with them unseen. These were coveted toys, and I was so desperate to have a GI Joe at any cost—to feel like a regular boy—that I pushed away the nagging thoughts in my conscience that what I'd just done was wrong.

When the neighbor boy asked me if I'd seen his action figures a few days later, I lied and said no. Once again my conscience bothered me, and I felt the burning guilt of my crime, but I never confessed to it. Even though Mom had taught us carefully not to lie or steal, at that moment I didn't care about the penalty I would pay or the beating I would receive if my mother ever found out.

The False Penitent

The years churned on, with my father in and out of our lives and startling changes happening in my own body. Suddenly my voice lowered to a new octave and I developed muscles that hadn't been there before. The reflection in the bathroom mirror showed a young man with new dark hair growth on his chin and upper lip.

By the time I turned thirteen, my experience in Santeria had reached new levels—I was learning how to control spirits to make them do my bidding, and visitors to the *centros* often sought me out for readings, recognizing the special gifting upon me to tell fortunes and break spells with complete accuracy. Yet for all my advancement in the world of witchcraft, I was still a boy craving the love of a father—an earthly father I had given up on.

Though my dad was rarely home, word of his escapades drifted back to us, twisting the knife in my gut with every fresh story. One evening he was hanging out with some friends at his buddy Manuel's house, drinking it up and listening to music. At some point late that night, after the others left, he and Manuel got into a disagreement about who was a better man—back and forth they compared themselves, regarding women and money and who drove the better car. As the argument escalated, suddenly my father jumped out of his seat and grabbed Manuel by the throat, choking the life out of him. Turning blue, in self-defense Manuel reached into his back pocket, grabbed an eight-inch knife, and plunged it into my father's stomach. My dad fell to the ground. Manuel called 911 and told the police my father came to the house looking for a fight, and he was forced to stab him in self-defense. An ambulance carted my father off to the hospital.

I never witnessed my dad getting in a fight. What he did in the street, he did in the street. But as time went on, he got even worse. He drank, mouthed off, and got into heated arguments that ended up in a lot of street brawls. Sometimes he was beat up badly and had to go to the hospital again. When we visited him, he made profuse promises to my mother that he was going to be a changed man. He announced dramatically, almost pitifully—gasping and wheezing because of his injuries—that he was going to stop drinking and playing around with other women. It almost seemed like he was repentant. And we all wanted so much to believe him.

"Esther, oh Esther, please forgive me! Give me another chance!" he would cough and plead in a ragged breath while holding onto my mother's hand. My brothers and I stood awkwardly to the side of his white hospital bed, watching the embarrassing scene. Once he even kissed her hand and double-kissed her wedding ring.

"I will make it up to you," he swore as a tear slid down the stubble on his cheek. It was the only time I ever saw any real tenderness from him. Deep inside I suspected his actions were prompted by being in the hospital and afraid to die—not out of any real love and concern for my mother. Because when he got better and the fire was back in his belly, as soon as his wounds healed, you could see his eyes dancing with plans, even from his hospital bed.

It was during those times, closest to his being released, that my father's remorseful behavior switched right in front of our eyes. He'd be sitting up in bed now, hair combed and gleaming with dressing oil, his face freshly shaved and cologne liberally applied. He was glorying in all the attention. At this point, he certainly didn't look sick or injured to me. I turned away, hiding my tears as I stared out the hospital window.

Once discharged from the hospital, of course nothing changed. If anything my father's drinking and hanging out became even more of his 24-7 obsession. There is a saying that "every dog has his day," and it's sad that it applied to my own father, but at this point his carousing had reached a fever pitch, one that was compelled to satisfy his most rabid carnal instincts no matter how it hurt everybody near and dear to him.

Farewell, My Father

One night my father was out with a drinking buddy at his favorite social club. Every poor neighborhood had a club like this one, an adult hangout where the liquor flowed and infidelities flourished. Details of that night only filtered back to me later, but the story goes that he was having a good old time with a barmaid, one of his many mistresses. As she served him his drinks, they flirted back and forth, with whispers, giggles, and cute talk. Apparently they had been lovers for a while, and my father lavished time, money, and attention on this good-time girl who had become one of his special girlfriends. Witnesses said she was wearing a low-cut top, skintight skirt, and fishnet stockings. She had been dancing around drunkenly, tottering on high heels, just a half hour before my dad entered the club.

While they flirted and laughed, a man entered the club, a stranger to my father who turned livid and purple when he recognized the woman my father canoodled with. As the stranger watched them flirt back and forth throughout the night, he became enraged. He started to pick a fight with my father's friend. Noticing the confrontation, the Great Eustaquio jumped up from his seat to shout at the stranger and defend his friend.

My father no doubt planned to just intimidate the stranger with the "evil eye" or a bare-knuckled defense if necessary. At the worst he would endure another ambulance-to-hospital stay, but either way he ultimately would be the barmaid's hero and resume their relationship.

The angry stranger had something final in mind. Without warning, in the middle of that escalating argument, he pulled out a piece of gray heavy metal from his black leather jacket. Unblinking, the stranger pulled the trigger and blasted a fiery gunshot into my shocked father's face, the bullet driving into his brain just above the eyebrow, killing him instantly. Pandemonium broke out in the bar, and the gunman fled into the night on foot and disappeared.

That night in our apartment, we heard a loud knock at the door as though someone were trying to break it down. As my mother opened the door, one of my father's sisters came in screaming hysterically "Eustaquio is dead! He just got shot…he's dead!"

Since I was the oldest, my mother grabbed me and we ran to the social club a block away. That night it rained like I had never seen before in a very mysterious way. It seemed as if heaven was crying and the sky was mourning. The raindrops fell heavy and hard like fifty-cent coins dropping from the sky. It rained nonstop. My mother and I stood in front of the social club wet and cold as my dad's body lay inside the smoke-filled room. As I watched the throng of policemen and curious onlookers surrounding the whole area, I asked myself why God was crying. Was it because my father lost his chance to go to heaven? I stood there, shivering from more than the cold rain, and tried to make the tears come, but my eyes and heart were empty.

Chapter 5

Nightmare on Crotona Avenue

I was thirteen when my father was killed, a sensitive age for a young boy with thoughts and intents and hormones changing, and now I had my ambivalence toward my father's death to contend with as well. All the bad thoughts I had toward him flooded my mind. All the times I had wished him dead came back for awhile to taunt me, because now he was dead.

At first I felt great guilt at my thoughts prior to his death. But soon, in realizing I didn't have to deal with him anymore, overwhelming relief washed over my guilt, and I felt absolutely no sadness. I felt my family's anguish had ended with my father's life, and my hardened thoughts tried to blot him out of my mind. My daily wish for his demise had finally come true. I thought then that the torment and hell would be over.

Later, I realized that the scars only covered my own internal injuries that would continue to haunt me. I grew to realize that the psychological wounds and my father's death were pivotal points that led me down a path of destruction that would twist my direction and change my life.

The next few years passed in a haze of struggles that my mother, brothers, and I constantly faced in our lives, trying to keep things afloat. The year after I turned sixteen, something good happened for once; 1980 turned out to be our lucky year. My mother's sister had lived in a beautiful area called East Fordham Road in the Bronx for a long time, and her landlord promised her that the next available apartment in his building would have our name on it. With our aunt's influence, it was the right price at the right time, and Mom had saved up enough from my father's Social Security checks to make the numbers work. For the first time, we looked forward to moving to the good side of town.

A Piece of Paradise

Fordham Road looked the way I always imagined "real" neighborhoods should be: clean, manicured streets lined with freshly painted stores—Woolworths, Alexander's department store, drugstores, grocery stores, an RKO Theater, Valentine's Theater, beautiful residential buildings, and—perhaps best of all—no ugly graffiti scrawled on everything in sight. It was a bustling, vibrant community, and we were proud to be a part of it. However, as only the fifth Hispanic family to move into the area, my brothers and I didn't know how to deal with the kids in the neighborhood because it was culture shock.

It came to a point where we had problems with the white kids in the area, many of whom were racist and wanted to beat us up. The first week we moved there they acted like they wanted to start a rumble. Every time we came outside they tried to chase us back into the building where we lived.

As my brothers and I walked to the corner store one day, here were the white kids hanging out in front of the candy store, taunting us and grouping together to try to set us up.

"Hey, spic!" one of the guys yelled. "We're coming after you. You think you can come in this neighborhood and just hang out on our corner?" The group of young men advanced on us, forming a semi-circle to come up at us from both sides.

I turned to my brothers and yelled, "Run, Julio! Run, George! Run as fast as you can!"

My brothers and I took off running—it was the third time in a week this had happened, and we left without getting to go inside the candy store.

Our Uncle Jimmy, an ex-gang member of the Reapers, decided to put things right on our behalf. He went and talked to the wannabe white hoodlums in the neighborhood. I heard about it secondhand that night at our apartment as he gloated over the way he scared them straight.

"It's like this," Jimmy said, jabbing the air for exaggerated effect, "I'll give you an ultimatum—either you leave my nephews alone or you're gonna have a fight on your hands. A real fight. If you're tough guys and really want to fight, I can come up here with some guys from the South Bronx and give you a rumble. You tell me what to do: We can call it peace or we can start a war."

The white kids decided to call it peace. A wise decision, no doubt. Eventually we became good friends with most of them and laughed about our initial standoff.

Since I was sixteen and the oldest, and with no father figure at home, I was becoming the man of the family. I was really young to shoulder such responsibility, but I wanted to make sure our lives stayed in this new sunnier place. My best friend's mother got me a job working in a supermarket after school, packing and delivering groceries. Months later a friend from the neighborhood approached me about a part-time job at a children's department store. It was a better opportunity to help my mother in a better way. I gave half the money I made to my mother and kept the rest.

Life settled into a good rhythm on Fordham Road, and best of all we had a real park to play baseball in—no more throwing catch in dirty vacant lots filled with broken glass and rusted car parts.

A Demon's Fury

One bright summer afternoon, my brothers and I grabbed our baseball gloves and ball and headed over to the park to play catch. As a follower of "the religion" I had learned years earlier about the laws of the spirit world, and the different spirits that ruled specific locations. Whenever I entered the park, I was supposed to cross my arms over my chest in tribute to the demon spirits that ruled the foothills and woods there. My brothers always stood in awe and fear, making sure I entered the park with reverence, because if not they feared they would be harmed as well as me. But today I had other things on my mind and sauntered through the gate without stopping to pay respect. In my conscience I felt the weight of those demons hovering over me, waiting for me to pay them respect, but I pushed it aside.

"Hey, John!" Eustaquio called out. "Did you forget?"

"Forget what?" I shot back. "Let's just play baseball…that's what we came here for."

My youngest brother looked uneasy, knowing how seriously I took my witchcraft rituals. "Okay, I just warned you—that's all I'm doing."

I shrugged him off. "Don't worry about it. Come on, let's get a game started." We rounded up a few other guys and decided to play a real game, not just catch. A handful of their friends took seats on the bleachers to watch the game. As it turned out, it was a baseball game nobody forgot.

Halfway through the game the sky turned dark as thunderclouds gathered overhead. We kept looking up at the sky, surprised to watch it turn from bright sunshine to dark so suddenly.

"Come on, play ball!" someone shouted from the bleachers. "Don't worry about the weather. You're one hit away from taking this inning."

"Batter up, batter up! Get a hit!" another guy yelled.

A violent gust of wind blew through the park, bending the tree branches as they rustled against one another. Suddenly a lightning bolt cracked the sky wide open, followed by a rumble of thunder so loud it shook the ground. Somebody screamed.

"Whoa, did you see that?" the pitcher yelled, but his voice got drowned out by another bolt, this time hitting the large oak tree near the baseball diamond. We heard the tree trunk splinter and crack as a guy from the opposing team ran to second base.

By now the wind had picked up even more, howling and whipping against our faces and tossing our hats off our heads. I knew the rain couldn't be far behind, and a downpour would surely end the game on the spot.

"Bring him home, bring him home!"

We all felt the adrenaline of the moment—the game was close, and one more run would give the opposing team the winning advantage. Meanwhile it seemed all hell was breaking loose in the sky overhead and the contorting trees around us.

Crack! The next guy up at bat hit a huge pop fly ball, but our outfielder missed it and dashed after the ball. The batter tore off running, yelling for his teammate on second base to bring it home.

"Home it, home it!" his teammates chanted, and as the guy on second rounded third and then slid into home base, his left leg twisted in a horribly unnatural position. I knew it was broken even before I heard him scream.

Instantly a cluster of guys surrounded the boy writhing on the ground at home base. Amid the crack of thunderbolts, the sky opened up, unleashing a torrent of rain over the ballpark.

"Let's get outta here!" one guy yelled, looking up at the angry sky. He and another teammate carried their wounded friend away, their backs bent against the lashing rain. The bleachers cleared out as the onlookers ran for cover, scattering to their cars and the picnic pavilions.

My brothers and I stood in silence as we watched the ballpark empty. At this point everything was gloomy and dark, as if nightfall had come early that day. Fear gripped us and our hearts pumped wildly, because we knew something supernatural was happening. We all felt it.

Eustaquio glared at me. "I told you, man! This is all your fault. I knew you should have done what you were supposed to do when we came into the park. You should have paid your respect! Now look at what's happened! It's your fault."

Julio and George stared at me sullenly, not saying a word. They didn't have to. I knew Eustaquio was right. My cavalier attitude had roused the anger of the spirits that day.

"I'm sorry!" I shouted to the heavens. "I'm sorry, I'm sorry!"

Back to the Gutter

The beautiful streets of East Fordham Road didn't last for long. Within two years my father's Social Security expired and we lost that income, which caused a huge reversal of fortune that forced our family back into the gutter. We said goodbye to East Fordham Road and in 1982 moved to the projects on Crotona Avenue, one of the toughest neighborhoods in the South Bronx. After Fordham Road, moving to Crotona Avenue was like moving into hell, but it was hell on earth.

Even the neighborhood looked like it was in pain because of the corruption and rundown buildings, where graffiti covered every concrete wall within reach. This was a place where you could touch the poverty. And always, hanging in the air over everything, was the ever-present reality of crime. Right next to the *bodega* (grocery store) on the corner, the Chinese takeout looked like a miniature Fort Knox. Every time you went for Chinese you didn't know whether you were going to get food or heading to the bank because of all the bars surrounding the place. Now we played baseball and football on a schoolyard concrete lot—no longer the lush green park of the East Bronx.

We lived a block away from the Bronx Zoo, and sometimes I wondered whether we needed to be caged up and the animals set free. The pent-up anger, frustration, and rebellion of those who lived in this neighborhood were contagious, and we caught the infection. Sometimes killings occurred at two o'clock in the afternoon, right out in the open. Without warning you'd walk by a crime scene on your way to the store and see where the police had taped down the corner. Or, worse, you would glimpse the body of a young man covered in a white sheet, nothing but his sneakers sticking out.

During our first few weeks there, all my brothers and I did was get into fights with guys from the neighborhood. In a tough neighborhood like the one we now lived in, someone always wanted to test you and see what you were made of, and my brothers and I were really tested. Whenever we came home from school, we never told Mom about all the fights because we knew she would worry. We tried our best to hide the cuts and bruises, making some lame excuse for why our bodies bore the marks of street violence. Eventually the neighborhood bullies got tired of fighting us, and we became friends. But being friends was worse than being enemies because every bad thing these guys did, we followed along just to fit in. Hey, who said there were any good boys in the hood? There were a few nice kids; they just weren't hip like us. And in time their parents moved away from the neighborhood so they wouldn't lose their children to the streets or watch them end up in jail.

My brothers and I knew there was no way out for us, so we adjusted to the environment of drug dealing, shootouts, muggings, stabbings, and death—which went on every day—by hanging out with school friends who lived in better neighborhoods. The violence in the neighborhood was out of control. One time involved a friend of mine who was very well-known with the drug dealers in the neighborhood. As he sat in his car at a stoplight, two guys drove up on a motorcycle. Before it was said and done, bullets rained into his car, cutting his life short. I was stunned by the news. Who would have thought his life would be over while waiting for a traffic light? That was life in the hood—alive today and dead tomorrow.

A Taste for Blood

My brother George ran upstairs to our apartment one day, shut himself in our room, and didn't come out for two days. When he finally came out, he paced the hall like a caged animal. I saw a crazed look in his eyes and knew something was wrong.

"What's going on, George? Why are you not acting right? Talk to me," I said, my voice coming out stern.

George avoided eye contact and kept pacing. "It's nothing, man. Forget it."

"I said talk to me—maybe it's something I can help you out with."

My brother snorted contemptuously. "Nobody can help me out of this, man. It's just...you know, I'm having problems with the guys on the corner over money, which I never took. Now they're trying to blame me for it, and

I didn't do anything. They're hunting me down like an animal."

With his words something clicked in my brain and rage consumed me. Now I started pacing back and forth. "Didn't I tell you not to hang out with these drug dealer losers?" I shouted. "All I'm gonna end up doing is going to your funeral. You're a loser just like our dad."

"Yeah, well, we're all losers one way or another," George shot back.

The next morning George finally decided to go outside. As he approached the corner of the building where we lived, a guy jumped out of a parked car and ran up behind him. As my brother turned around, the guy shot at him five times. All five bullets missed him. When I heard the news, I knew that the demons I catered to—the demons I served—protected my brother. In that instant I also understood my mission and assignment from hell was to put my brother in jail, where he would be safe, not stand by and watch him end up in the cemetery. That day my powers increased in the demon world, and I set out with a vengeance to destroy the life of the person who tried to kill my brother.

I challenged the devil, yelling out loud, "You better do something or else! That person better die! Do you hear me?"

His answer came quiet my spirit: "I will avenge my fury and anger on that person, and you will hear all about it. Then you will truly know that I am your dad." A few weeks later, the person who tried to murder my brother was killed in the street like the dog he was.

Unfortunately, drug dealers run in packs, and I knew the dead guy had buddies who still wanted their money—or my brother's life. Jail was the safest place he could be, so I summoned the demons to inquire what to do to put him there. The demons sent me to the four corners of the neighborhood to collect dirt from the place where my brother used to hang out with his boys.

I went and got two roosters and chopped off their heads because I needed the sacrificial blood for the power to cast this spell on my brother. It gave me pleasure to chop the struggling roosters' heads off, wishing they were my brother's enemies instead. Next I wrote his name on the inside of a brown paper bag, wrapped it up, and put it in a dark bottle with the dirt of the four corners. Finally I turned it over to the devil and placed it in the cauldron— a cast-iron pot where the devil and his demons meet. Strangely turned on by the killings, and watching the blood drip from the roosters' necks, I knew my witchcraft powers were increasing all the more. Within twenty-four hours my brother George was in jail.

But not everyone I knew escaped death so easily. Several months later, two cousins who made their living selling drugs got into a territory fight that ended in a bloodbath. One of the cousins was better at the game than the other. Late one night, Gary decided to make extra money while his cousin Ron was away. He decided to go into Ron's turf and sell drugs to his customers. To Gary's surprise, across the street a cab suddenly pulled into the curb and out of the cab came Ron. As Ron spotted Gary, he pulled out his 9mm gun and fired away, spraying bullets until Gary hit the ground. Ron crossed the street and finished him off.

Early the next morning my brother George ran upstairs and told us the news. As soon as I heard, I ran out to where the killing took place. A cluster of police cars blocked the crime scene, but as I peeked through the swarm of officers and medical personnel, I saw the blood-stains on the pavement.

Oddly, in that moment, the only thing that crossed my mind was the pool of blood that was wasted—blood I could have used for witchcraft. How I regretted not being there to collect that blood before it seeped into the asphalt.

Chapter 6

A Night of Voodoo

The devil was on a mission. Although I had been a practicing warlock for nearly ten years now, it was time to go deeper. Unseen forces pulled me into new levels of evil I had only heard about previously. Voices talked in my head, and my waking and dreaming hours blurred with strange visions. Satan was reminding me that I had a contract to fulfill and I belonged to him.

One night I fell asleep and felt myself pulled into a bizarre dream—it seemed more real than my waking reality, so real I got sucked into the dream and didn't know whether I was dreaming or actually there at that very moment. I woke up in a cold sweat, jumped out of bed, and looked around the room, my breath coming in gasps. Nothing was there. I glanced across the room and saw my brother George asleep in his bed. Outside, the familiar nighttime Bronx sounds filtered through the dingy windowpanes. Deciding it was just a nightmare, I crawled back under the covers and soon fell asleep. This time I found myself by the ocean, and I knew that *Madre Agua*—the spirit that rules the ocean—was talking to me by the edge of the water. I could hear the waves rush into shore and then whoosh back out to sea. Overhead, the sky was lit by a million twinkling stars. When she spoke, I heard her voice resonating in my spirit: "I am your mother in the religion. I am the one who will guard you and protect you. You need to step out and bring people to the religion so you can have your own village of people. You have been chosen and called for this."

Madre Agua stood tall and serene against the crystal blue water, dressed in a white gown that was transparent and flowed far below where her feet should have been as she floated above the ground. She wore a necklace around her neck made out of seashells, and her long black hair flowed in the wind, framing her angelic face. But despite her beauty I could feel that she was fearless and very dangerous.

"Thank you for the blessing, thank you for revealing yourself to me," I stammered. "I will do my very all to accomplish what I was called to do."

Instantly I woke up, startled once again from the strange, vivid dream, not knowing where I was for a moment and trying to gather my thoughts. When my eyes settled on the familiar furniture of my bedroom, I realized something curious—though I was at home in my bed, I could still smell the ocean brine, it was so real.

Pulled back into sleep again, this time I woke up high on a mountain in the deepest part of the forest. Towering trees surrounded me on all sides, and I felt the spongy forest floor beneath my feet. Right in front of me, between two trees, stood a big Indian chief spirit, maybe nine or ten feet tall. As I looked at him, I knew it was Tawata, my main protective spirit, the one who threw the beaded necklace out of the sky for me to wear when I was nine years old.

"*Mi padre,*" I said at once, awed by his presence. "What is this all about?"

The tall spirit gazed at me for a few seconds before he spoke. "You have been called to the world of spiritualism, and I'm the one who is going to guide you where no other human being has walked before. You will have my powers to tell people all about their lives, their destinies, and their purpose. It is time to get started."

Burning Flesh

Fueled by the strange but powerful dreams, I started attending even more occult gatherings, including parties at the *centros* to honor the demons who gave us our powers. These festive celebrations resembled birthday parties, except there was nothing innocent about them. What went on in these gatherings was pure evil. One of the most demonic initiations used by *espiritismo* was the cigar burning.

One Friday evening after midnight, Aunt Maria got demon-possessed by a spirit who called herself the mother of Haiti—the principality that guards Haiti. Speaking through my aunt, the demon spirit requested dark rum and a cigar. Somebody brought the liquor to her in a coconut shell, and I watched as my aunt lit the cigar and puffed on it until the coal turned red-hot. Her eyes dark with purpose, Aunt Maria called three of us to the front, including me. Speaking in her demonic language, she said, "We're going to see tonight who truly belongs to us, and this ceremony will determine that."

The cigar kept turning redder and redder. The other two, a man and an older woman, went first. The man was told to lift up the back of his shirt. As he kneeled on the floor in front of my aunt, she plunged the lit cigar into the bare skin on his back. He screamed like someone trapped in hell as she branded him in different parts of his back. Finally, he passed out.

Quivering with fear, the woman came forward next. Aunt Maria commanded her to close her eyes and extend her arm. When my aunt plunged the cigar into the woman's wrist, she too screamed and fainted.

At last she approached me and told me to hold out my arm and close my eyes. As I stuck out my arm, I felt the heat of the cigar approaching my skin like a flaming torch. She pressed the red-hot coal into my arm and held it there, searing my flesh. I locked my teeth and squeezed my eyes shut tight, allowing the cigar to remain on my skin, because I knew I was called to do this. I overcame the pain and the smell of my own burning flesh—and that night I knew I was one of them.

"John," Aunt Maria called as I started to head for home later that night. She gestured for me to step into the hallway apart from the others. "There's a secret meeting Monday night, and I want you to be a part of it," she said, her voice lowered. "Only the proven ones can be there, and tonight you proved yourself."

"What's the meeting about?"

"This is for high-ranked mediums in the religion, and we're gathering to map out the coming year, to find out which principalities are going to run which regions. We're also going to punish those that dared to come against us," she said, a devilish smile painted across her face. I knew it was time for war.

I went about my business over the next few days in high expectations for what Monday night would bring. We gathered at Aunt Maria's house in the basement. Glancing around the candlelit room, I realized I was standing among a select group of mediums who had ominous powers. The meeting's purpose: to settle the score and counter-attack our enemies, a group of people who wanted to make a name for themselves and tried to do witchcraft on one of our people. But we caught it, and it was time to teach them a lesson.

Earlier that day my aunt had purchased a dozen dark-colored roosters for the purpose of sacrificing—we needed their blood to do the witchcraft. That night, we all gathered together prepared to do war. As the conga players started beating the drums near the front of the gathering, the atmosphere was set and I felt the spirits of *espiritismo* enter the room to receive the sacrifices. The presence grew heavy; thick darkness hovered over the basement as the smell of cigars and rum perfumed the air. The hair on my arms and the back of my neck stood up as I felt shadows passing by.

We chanted as the conga players beat the drums harder. Some sang, some danced to the demons, others lit up cigars and blew smoke while still others sprayed rum on the four corners of the basement floor, with the symbols of *espiritismo* in the center of it. Every now and then a small explosion lit the room as somebody poured alcohol on the concrete floor and threw a burning match on it. In time we felt hell arrive in that basement. Even the roosters, squawking from their cages, knew that evil danced in the air. You could see terror in their eyes, as if they knew they were going to die.

As the music played the energy in the room got heavier and heavier, and I knew that in just a matter of days our enemies would pay. Aunt Maria distributed the voodoo recipe of what we needed to do to chasten those who betrayed us. I had a taste for blood that night—my heart was pumping fast and my knife was sharp, ready to behead a few roosters. I was excited to be one of those chosen to kill the roosters. Grabbing one after another by its feet, I plunged the knife into the roosters' necks and drained their blood. When I was done, claws and feet and beheaded necks were scattered all over the basement floor. The demons cackled with delight through the mediums who lent them their bodies for the ritual, their demonic laughter mingling with the screams of the birds. Blood dripped from my hands, and if I'd had the chance to lick my hands I would have, but what would the others think? As we came down to the last rooster I opened its mouth and stuck the sharp edge of the blade right down its throat with hate and anger, knowing that the blood was a contract and the killing would destroy someone else's life.

I came out of that secret meeting feeling giddy with power—wicked energy all over me—and celebrating the victory that was about to take place. Sometime later we heard that the house of our enemies caught fire and burned to the ground. They became homeless and had nowhere to stay. I knew they learned a hard lesson not to mess with fire, because *we* were fire.

The drawing to the dark side seemed to be getting stronger. All this made me hang out more with my friends and brought on more drinking, more women, more clubbing, and now sex. I started to get a hunger for the club scene. I was living like my dad without realizing it. The life that I hated him for had now become my life. The curse upon my father had not only reached me but was now taking over my brothers as well. My mother couldn't do anything to stop it. We were out of control and headed in the direction my father had once lived. Now she had four sons that reminded her of the abusive-drinking husband she had lost. Old doors and wounds had been reopened.

Graveyard Ritual

Fall came and with it a chill wind blew through the Bronx, forcing its residents to layer up and lean into the cold air as they made their way down the noisy city streets. For me, autumn meant one thing—the approach of Halloween, my favorite holiday. Halloween is the most mysterious, carnal, and devilish holiday of them all. I always laughed at those who celebrated Halloween by changing their identity for one night, and those who claimed to be witches and warlocks because they danced around in front of open fires set in a field or forest beneath a full moon. To me they were fools, like little kids playing with matches, not realizing the thing they played with had the power to kill. I knew the real meaning of this black holiday: Halloween is the night to have the most demonic powers available to use to kill and destroy those you hate.

The week before Halloween, I prepared for a special assignment to do just that—inflict suffering and death on three people I was contracted to destroy. That Wednesday night, St. Ilia, the demon spirit that owns the gates of the cemetery, instructed me to visit the tombs of those who had died recently so I could capture their spirits.

My second godmother in the religion, a one-of-a-kind witch, met up with me and we walked the fifteen blocks to the walled cemetery. No one lurked about as we approached the wrought-iron gates of the cemetery. As usual, the gates were locked after sundown, so my godmother waited by the gates while I paid my respect with twenty-one pennies, then climbed the wall to leap over. As I stood on the wall, I gazed into a sea of concrete tombstones and was in awe. The statues of different saints distinguished different parts of the cemetery—even the place of the dead was beautiful.

I roamed the tombs. It was fresh graves I sought, not old ones—graves only weeks old. Directed by St. Ilia, I visited three graves that night—two that had committed suicide and one that was shot to death. My assignment was to take those spirits home to use them against my enemies, and those people would die the same way the ones in the graves had died. It was cold. The ground of those tombs felt like ice as I knelt before each one and carried out the contract, using the pieces of white candles, a cigar, and white rum I had brought.

"John, is everything okay?" my godmother croaked in a hoarse voice from the cemetery gates.

"Yeah, yeah, everything's okay. Just leave me alone…I'm doing my thing," I said, irritated that she might raise a disturbance.

"I just wanted to make sure you were okay," she replied.

"What a stubborn person I brought with me tonight," I muttered under my breath. But my irritation soon gave way to excitement as the demon spirit led me from grave to grave. I shivered. I didn't know whether I was cold because of the weather or because I was surrounded by the dead that night. My veins pumped with adrenaline as I realized that in just a few days Halloween would be at my door; I was going to go out and have a good time with my boys—my enemies long forgotten.

Halloween Rendezvous

That weekend, on Halloween night, I catered to the demons at my home, set up all my witchcraft spells against those I hated, and then got dressed up and went to meet my two friends at the neighborhood club in Parkchester.

We were too cool to be dressed in costumes. Instead I wore a nice pair of jeans, a white shirt, and had my hair slicked back to perfection. We could hear the music pumping loudly as we approached the club on foot.

"Hey, John, you gonna meet some cuties tonight?" my buddy Jose said, nudging me with his elbow. "I can feel it, bro. I can feel the vibes."

"Oh yeah?" I grinned back at him. "Maybe I will— I'll try to find one for both of you's too." We laughed as we paid the cover charge and stepped past the bouncer into the darkened club. Inside the scene was electric, with a few hundred people all dressed out in crazy costumes and the dance floor packed with bodies gyrating to the salsa beat. The atmosphere was right. I could feel the eerie Halloween chill in the air, and I knew the spirits wanted to communicate with me. I didn't know whether to party that night or look for victims.

I saw her in the corner—a beautiful girl in a short, black, elegant witch costume with long black hair and pale skin. She had the face of an angel, and instantly I knew I had to have her. Whoever she was, she didn't have a problem saying no, as I saw guy after guy get shot down when they asked her to dance. But somehow I knew it would be different for me, even though I was shy about approaching her.

Go to her, a voice in my head commanded. *She's yours.*

I sauntered across the room and stood right next to her at the bar. Her back was turned to me as she talked with her girlfriend.

"Would you like to dance?" I asked over the music.

She turned around, and a slow smile spread across her beautiful face. "I would love to," she said. As we danced on the dance floor, we kept gazing at each other and smiling.

"What's your name?" I said, leaning my head down close to her ear.

"I'm Mari...I live in Brooklyn."

"Well, you're a long way from home, Mari, but I'm glad you decided to come to the Bronx tonight. I'm John. I hope we can get to know each other better."

"We'll see," she said, tossing her hair with a coy smile.

We kept dancing all night, and at one point I felt the spirits telling me to kiss her. Without warning I leaned over and kissed her full on the mouth, and she went into shock—she even stopped dancing for a few seconds, at a loss for words. I did it for shock effect and it worked. As I leaned back I gave her a devilish smile.

When the club closed I walked Mari to her car. We stood there for a few moments, both caught up in the mysterious night and not wanting it to end.

"How can I stay in contact with you?" I asked her finally. She wrote her number on a piece of paper and gave it to me. I nodded, memorizing the numbers as soon as I read them. "I'll stay in touch, and thanks for the evening. I had a wonderful night."

As Mari got into her car, I closed the door for her and watched her drive away. Walking on my way home into the night, I felt mystical, excited—and I was already planning my next move.

Chapter 7

Jekyll & Hyde

In the fall of 1987 Mari and I were geared up and looking forward to a Halloween wedding, but not just any wedding. The union of our souls on that witches' holiday—exactly two years from the night we met—was the perfect night for this dark ceremony that would bind us together not in the sight of God but in the sight of Satan.

A fellow warlock in the religion offered the use of his basement for the ceremony, and as the calendar moved toward October 31 I felt excitement stirring in my veins. In twenty-five years, only two previous weddings had been performed like the one about to take place. That's how diabolical the commitment of an *espiritismo* wedding was; most others didn't dare to take those vows. Word spread about the evil nature of our upcoming wedding, and none of my family or Mari's family attended, so we had a separate traditional ceremony for them to attend.

Stepping into the basement that night was like stepping into hell, with the atmosphere on fire—not only from the people attending but from the different spirits gathered there to witness the diabolical wedding taking place that night. The basement was decorated with twenty-one colorful handkerchiefs representing the twenty-one paths of the dark side. An altar made out of leaves and tree branches stood at the front and center of the room. As we waited for the ceremony to begin, my heart pounded as I knew what was about to take place really *was* a ceremony of "till death do us part."

Aunt Maria, possessed by the demon principality that ruled Haiti, stood in front of the altar and leveled her dark eyes at us. "The ceremony is about to begin—there's no turning back!" the demon inside her shouted, her voice guttural-sounding.

Mari and I both wore the protective colors of our main demon spirits—she in a blue and white cape, and I in a red cape. Aunt Maria sprayed rum and blew cigar smoke on the wedding bands, lit them on fire, then turned to me and said, "Do you agree with the contract?" I said yes. Then she turned to Mari and said, "Do you agree with the contract?" and she said yes. In that moment the contract was sealed. After the ceremony two candles—male and female figures in white—were united face to face, tied up with red and white thread, and buried under the ground at the back of the house.

Twenty-one people with different ranks of powers stood on either side of the altar to bless the wedding. It was a wedding of demons, *congos*, *negros*, *madamas*, *indios*, and gypsies that came down that night to celebrate and prophesy about our marriage. We celebrated until five in the morning.

A Date with the Unknown

As I stared into the eyes of Mari, my new bride, I remembered the first tarot card reading I took her to two years earlier—her first encounter with *espiritismo*. That night I had taken her through the first door, and she didn't realize the magnitude of what she was getting involved with. Like most people, Mari did not know that card reading was one of the twenty-one paths to the occult. My father's side of the family had been sold out to the religion, something that looked spiritual on the outside, but in reality they were all devil worshippers who claimed to be living for God.

The tarot card reading came about easily, naturally, not long after Mari and I met on Halloween night at the club. One day as we grabbed lunch at a diner, Mari's sister Carmen sighed loudly across the table, catching our attention.

"What's wrong?" Mari asked.

"I just don't know what to do," Carmen said, shaking her head. "I'm going crazy—it's been three days since he called, Mari! Three days!"

"Give it time. He'll come around," Mari said nonchalantly.

"Who'll come around," I asked.

"Miguel, that guy she met at the club the same night we met," Mari said, smiling up at me. "Don't you remember her dancing all night with that one guy?"

"Nah, my eyes were only on you." I reached over and kissed her cheek, and she nestled closer against my chest.

I looked across the table at Carmen. "I know a way you can find out how it's going to end up. My aunt does card readings, and she can tell you whether you're wasting your time with this guy or not."

"For real?" Carmen stared at me, her eyes round with interest. "Are you serious? 'Cause if you mean it, sign me up. I can't stand not knowing any longer."

"I can take you there in the next couple of days if you want to go."

"I want to go too!" Mari said, her voice filled with excitement. I smiled at her, pleased to see how eager she was to enter my world.

"Yeah, yeah, sure...I can get both of you's appointments for a card reading. It will be good for both of you— you'll see."

The night I brought Mari and Carmen for their tarot card reading, they came with lighthearted spirits, expecting answers for Carmen and a good time for Mari. But what they thought was going to be fun turned bad when they both were exposed for lies they had told me.

At my aunt's house that evening, we all sat on the sofa anticipating who was going to go first with the card reading. They kept giggling and saying, "You go first"... "no, you go first," because although they were excited, they were also very nervous.

"I bet my card reading is going to be better than yours," Mari teased.

"Oh, yeah?" Carmen shot back. "No, listen, mine's going to be better than yours...mine's going to be peaches and cream. I know that for a fact. And yours is gonna be rough!"

I jumped into the conversation. "What if you both are in for a big surprise tonight?" They turned and stared at me, their dark brown eyes serious and troubled for a minute before they burst into giggles again. Eventually Aunt Maria called Mari into the back room to do her reading. I stayed out front, but Mari shared the details later about what went on in the back room.

As Mari looked on intently, she watched Aunt Maria prepare herself for the tarot card reading. She reached for her bottle of perfume and ceremoniously cleaned herself then turned her dark, lifeless eyes onto Mari and held out the perfume bottle with a dim grin. "Now it's your turn."

That night Mari's life would never be the same as my aunt told her to cut the deck of cards in three—past, present, and future. As the first deck was laid out, the nightmare began for Mari, with Aunt Maria telling her about her childhood, her broken home, and the dysfunctional family she was brought up in. As Mari heard my aunt speak these words, not knowing a thing about her past, she choked and tried to hold back her tears. Aunt Maria went into the second deck of cards, and that's when the gypsy spirit dug deeper into Mari's soul and exposed the charade she had going with Carmen.

"You and your so-called sister Carmen, you aren't really sisters are you?" Aunt Maria said, her black eyes penetrating through Mari like she was transparent.

Mari looked at her in despair, swallowed hard, and with a small voice said, "No, we aren't."

"And you also have a live-in boyfriend," Aunt Maria continued, smirking. "You're a pretty good liar. Does my nephew know about this?"

Mari looked down, not daring to look Aunt Maria straight in the eye, and with a small whisper she said, "No."

Suddenly my aunt stood up from the chair, glared down at Mari, and pointed her long finger at her face. "I am a high-ranked witch. If anything were to happen to my nephew, if even a hair is missing from his head, I will destroy you piece by piece and your family one by one with my powers, and I will send you straight to hell," she said, her voice low and cunning. "So we're going to call John into the room right now. This card reading has come to an end, and you will tell him everything."

And that's exactly what they did. Before that night was over, I learned everything there was to know about Mari, her secret boyfriend, and the girl who claimed to be her sister. From that point on, Aunt Maria and I formed a tight relationship because that was the night I made a pact with the devil and the power of *espiritismo*.

I loved having the power to control and the idea of pretending to be one person, yet being another. It was like leading a double life. It drew me closer and more involved in a relationship with the devil and his demons. That night Mari decided she would break up with her live-in boyfriend, but only if I forgave her and was willing to commit myself to a serious relationship with her. I said yes to both. Mari's first decision was to move in with her mother, and her friend Carmen supported the idea.

Mari stayed with her mom for awhile and sometime later moved in with me and my family in the housing projects. She and I stayed there for a short time until we saved enough money for our own apartment. We went out in the evenings and worked hard by day, fixing up our new apartment with style. Between the furniture, the freshly painted walls, and the artwork we had chosen, our place became one-of-a-kind. Friends and family loved it every time they came to visit.

Things were going so well we knew we were destined to be together. After dating for awhile, Mari came out one day and said, "John, I think we should get married on Halloween." We had talked about it back and forth but never made serious plans before. "We met on Halloween, so it's a perfect day to tie the knot. What do you think?"

I didn't hesitate a second. "Wow, that sounds like a great idea. That's the day we'll get married then."

Later, Mari and I also attended secret ceremonies and witchcraft parties held in people's basements or apartment houses. She got pulled into the religion gradually, over time, because of the excitement it had to offer. Here was something totally different in her life—different from being Catholic. In her mind it was just white magic; black magic was only used when she needed to defend herself— at least that's how she justified it. This demonic world of *espiritismo* and Santeria is very much like the military, which consists of ranks. From a very young age I already had a high rank in the religion. Now it was my wife's turn to climb the ranks.

Recruiting newcomers intrigued us because we used the power of evil to do it. My aunt and I knew hundreds of people who became members of the occult: doctors, nurses, police officers, lawyers, judges, school principals—the list was endless. Anyone who wanted to join was invited, blue- and white-collar workers alike. Recruiting people was my second stage into the dark side.

A Precious Gift

My wife and I were happily married, and in 1988 she became pregnant. It was a great year for both of us. I was so thrilled I was going to be a father, and my family too was happy to hear that a child was on the way.

Throughout that year things went pretty normal for Mari and me. We both had jobs, and so every morning I would drive her to work and pick her up at the end of the day because of her condition. She was a great wife and I was a good husband. We managed very well in our marriage and our everyday life.

Before I knew it, in June 1989, Mari gave birth to a twenty-two-inch-long, six-pound baby girl. Being in the delivery room was a great experience for me, and our daughter, whom we named Amanda, was a gift to my wife and me. While Mari stayed home to take care of the baby, I kept working to cover the expenses of the home. But later, when she felt it was time to go back to work, a conflict arose as to who would take care of our daughter. We had two choices: It would either be my mother, who lived near us in the Bronx, or her mother, who lived far away in Brooklyn. Mari decided her mother would be the babysitter, which made it difficult because of the commute I would have to make every day back and forth to Brooklyn. But despite that, our marriage was good day in and day out.

With our work schedules, we made a lot of money and saved a lot too, because I knew from the moment our relationship got serious that as soon as the holidays came around there would be strong disagreements between us about buying expensive gifts for our families. And that's exactly what happened.

Spending holiday time with Mari's family was okay with me. I always enjoyed myself and they treated me well. But later when I wanted to spend the holidays with my relatives, Mari did not understand. Neither did she want to share her life with my side of the family. So because of this we had strong disagreements whenever any of the major holidays came around, and no one was to blame but me. From the very beginning I had agreed to do every Christmas and Thanksgiving with her family, and that took away from our marriage, even though we still loved each other. We gave Amanda the very best: good clothes, private schools, and a good upbringing. And every year, whether it was Easter, Christmas, or her birthday, we gave her many gifts. But we kept that "other" thing we did as a couple very private from our families.

Dancing with Demons

The endless round of underworld parties and feasts and spiritual celebrations we took part in as members of the religion filled our lives to the brim, but we loved every minute of it—being part of something bigger than ourselves. Sometimes Mari and I attended meetings to summon dead relatives. In other gatherings, demons showed up and would speak of themselves: their birthdays, their favorite foods, what colors they liked, how they lived, and what part of the world they inhabited in their past life. They required special celebrations in their honor, and like obedient pawns we did their every bidding.

Late one evening, Mari and I received an invitation to go to a spiritual feast to celebrate the birthday of a particular demon who claimed to be born as a gypsy in the mid-1700s in Spain. She was very rich, very beautiful, and very powerful when she walked the earth, she claimed.

Men adored her, and she was beheaded at the hands of a jealous man at the age of thirty-two. The gathering took place at my aunt's basement. A string quartet dressed in Spanish garb had been hired to play classical music, and the basement was decked out with flowers and eighteenth-century decorations.

Champagne flowed all night long at this classy black-tie event, but despite the refined music and fancy clothing, debauchery and promiscuity studded the atmosphere because that's what this particular demon spirit was all about. This feast, which only came around once a year, was a time to dance promiscuously, touch lasciviously, and cross boundaries.

I glanced around the room and noticed the mirrors were left uncovered. Normally, whenever we had demonic parties, the host covered the mirrors because the demon spirits could not look at themselves (or rather the reflection of the human they possessed that night) in the mirrors. But this spirit—the beautiful Spanish gypsy—earned the privilege of staring at herself in the mirror.

The demon had so completely taken possession of Aunt Maria that night that her features changed to the likeness of the Spanish woman from the mid-1700s. My aunt wore a costume gown from the era the demon spirit lived in, made particularly for that feast and only to be worn that night and never again. When she smiled at her reflection in the mirror, it was no longer Aunt Maria looking back from the glass—I saw the features of another woman from another time. Immersed though I was in this dark underworld of *espiritismo*, even I felt a chill run down my spine.

Trouble in Paradise

Often as I lay in my bedroom watching TV, Amanda would come and crawl into bed next to me, curl up against my side as a little two-year-old, and we would watch TV together. In her toddler mind she would ask me silly questions that would make me laugh and bring joy to my life.

"Daddy, what cartoon is coming up next?" she would ask.

"The Power Rangers are coming on next."

"The red one is my favorite," she said. "Daddy, which one do you like?"

"I like the blue one," I said, grinning down at her.

"No, Daddy, you have to like the red one, that's the one I like."

And I would say, just to tease her, "No, you like the red one, I like the blue one."

"Then we're not watching the Power Rangers 'cause you don't like the red one!" she would say, and then burst into giggles.

I grabbed her and tickled her and said, "Okay, I like the red one…we'll watch the Power Rangers."

I often wonder in the back of my mind if my dad ever took time out and sat with me and did the same things I stopped to do with my daughter—because I have no memory of such things.

When Amanda was two years old, I got a tattoo on my arm of an angel with her name on it. But my daughter disliked the picture on my arm.

"Daddy, the angel is naked," she said one day, pointing her finger at my arm. "Please put clothes on it."

"It's supposed to be that way, Amanda," I said.

And she said, "No, Daddy, take it back to the man that did it. Tell him to put some clothes on the angel."

I burst out laughing, because all her sayings were cute and innocent to me. She made a pouty face, and I just grabbed her and kissed her and told her, "One day you will understand why Daddy got the tattoo, because this is how much he loves you."

Apart from our nighttime round of demonic activities, my wife and I lived a normal life with our daughter. We looked like the all-American young couple, living the high life and destined for good things. But already cracks were forming in the foundation of our marriage.

There were many weekends that Mari and I did great things together, but other times she started going out with her friends while I stayed home with Amanda. We had an agreement that some weekends she would go out with her friends and I would stay home with Amanda. But when I wanted to go out with the guys, she would start a fight because she didn't want to be left home by herself with our daughter. To solve this, we got a babysitter, but now when we went out we went our separate ways—she with her friends and I with the guys. We agreed to get home by the same time, no later than four in the morning, which worked out very well for a while.

One night it was my turn to go out; Mari had gone out the night before.

As I sat on the living room sofa channel-surfing, she came and stood right in front of me, her hands on her hips. "You need to drive me to the grocery store today so I can buy some things for the house," she stated flatly.

I leaned around her and continued staring at the TV screen. "You know how to drive, so drive yourself. I want to rest up a bit so I can go out with the guys tonight."

"So the guys are more important than our marriage? Is that how it is now?"

"You know that's not so!" I shot back. "But you also know it's my turn to go out tonight. I'm going to rest, so if you want to buy some stuff you go out and get it yourself."

"You know what, I change my mind. I'm not gonna get *anything* for the house. You can get it yourself."

"What do I care?" I said, rising from the couch and throwing the remote on the sofa. "Leave it the way it is. It makes no difference to me." I turned around, went into the bedroom, and slammed the door shut.

That night I stepped out with my friends, and even though I had a good time, I still had Mari and Amanda on my mind. I couldn't be at ease knowing they were at home alone, because I loved them both. These thoughts rushed through my mind: *You're just like your dad.* So that night, instead of coming home at four in the morning, I walked into the house at 2:30 a.m. As I turned into the room, both of them were sound asleep. I kissed them both and went to sleep on the couch.

The holidays were upon us, and Mari and I agreed that on the weekend we would take some time out to go Christmas shopping to buy some gifts for our families. She chose items for her relatives, and I started to pick out gifts for my family. But she thought my family should get gifts for half the price of her family.

"Why should your family get the better gifts?" I said, trying not to make a scene.

Mari rolled her eyes. "Because my family is better than your family, that's why."

"Whoever told you that? They're both the same."

"Well, my family's done more things for our marriage than your family."

By now my voice was getting louder. "Well, the reason why is because you don't allow my family to do anything for our marriage!" A store clerk glanced at us as she straightened the shelves. Embarrassed, I muttered, "Here, whatever…I don't care what you buy." I put the items I had selected back on the shelf. So we left the store that day upset, and we decided to shop on our own different schedules for our respective families.

We came to a point in our marriage where we disagreed about anything and everything. We were exhausted in our marriage, and it wore us out to the point where we stopped trying. In the end we decided to go our separate ways. I came home from work one Friday evening after twelve hours of work, exhausted, and we weren't talking to each other.

Mari walked into the living room, her face devoid of expression, and uttered these words: "I'm leaving you and moving to my mother's tomorrow. You can stay with the apartment. I'm taking Amanda with me, and I think we should get a divorce."

I was dumbfounded, speechless, too tired to fight. I sat at the TV, channel-surfing, no words coming out of my mouth. The next evening, I sat in my living room with a beer in my hand staring around at the four walls, hitting the rewind button of my life, and wondering how I had ended up here in this situation—not only losing my wife, but losing my daughter. Tears flowed down my face, a pain you couldn't describe ripping my heart. I finally understood that there is no difference between a divorce and the death of a beloved relative. The pain is the same.

Eventually I came to the conclusion that I needed to take full responsibility for my marriage, because as a young man, not having a father figure or a person with a good marriage to coach me, I allowed my marriage to get to the point that it got. And maybe that's one of the reasons why Mari and I are not married today.

Haunted by Memories

The next day I found myself alone in the apartment in the Bronx we had once shared so happily. Now it had become a place of torment. Day after day and night after night accusing thoughts bombarded my mind. I felt like a loser after the divorce, just like my dad. I would miss the precious moments of watching my daughter grow. I wondered what my ex-wife would say when Amanda asked, "Where is my daddy?" "Why isn't he home?" "Why isn't he putting me to bed?"

My mind was in turmoil. I kept hearing my daughter's voice repeatedly asking questions. "When I wake up in the morning, why is my daddy not here?" "Why did my daddy leave me?" "I guess he doesn't love me anymore." "Will he ever come back?" and most of all, "I miss my daddy!"

I could imagine her mom's response. Mari would probably say, "He won't be coming home anymore, for you or for me, Amanda." Suddenly I hated witchcraft because it had robbed me of precious time with my daughter. I hated the world, I hated everything, but I loved my Amanda. If she only knew how much I loved her, and still do to this very day, more than I love myself. I would give my life for her anytime. I have all our memories treasured in my heart. Her being a little girl, carrying her in my arms, holding her hand everywhere we went. Amanda knew that every time she was with her daddy, she was well protected, even though at times I counted myself as a failure in her life. My love for her was always the same.

At nights I would lie in bed and wish and pray not to wake up the next morning because the pain was beyond any pain I had ever known.

What was the point of living?

Chapter 8

Losing It All

Time went on and Amanda grew. But we didn't grow apart. I went to all her birthday parties, spent Easter, Thanksgiving, and Christmas with her, and was allowed to see her on weekends. But being the dad I was I wanted more, and when I couldn't get it, it left me feeling confused, angry, and lost. The result: I pushed myself deeper into *espiritismo*. I immersed myself in a world of witchcraft parties, cleansing ceremonies, tarot card readings, and promotions to higher demonic ranks, learning new secrets. I liked learning more about the religion. How demons liked things done for them. Which ones liked blood and which ones preferred roosters or birds. I learned the different languages demons spoke so I could understand them. It was something like those "Hallelujah people" who spoke in a strange language themselves.

Higher levels brought new challenges and new skills. Each time I predicted someone's future, my powers increased, and with each increase unsuspecting people fell prey to whatever I told them—things only they knew about. This left them in awe, allowing me to do what I had done to others—reach down into their souls and drain them of their only means of protection: the power to resist the dark forces of *espiritismo*. Recruiting souls became my passion, a mission I lived to fulfill daily for the spirits I served.

By this point, my nightlife at the clubs was out of control. As much as I wanted to stop, a power stronger than me kept dragging me back. The clubs became like a playground for me. It was there that I started to recruit people into the dark side, introducing them to the religion. It was an addiction that kept me out many nights until the next morning.

I always hoped those I came across were the so-called Christians. They were my favorites. I was eager to challenge their "faith" and what they believed to be the truth. By getting them to agree to do a fortune reading, they allowed me to usher them through an open door to the satanic world. I exposed them to an evil they had no idea of, an evil that would bring all sorts of misfortune upon their lives. They always thought they had it all together and were better than others, and that the world I lived in was not good enough for them. How I hated hearing them talk about this man called Jesus and how much He loved them. To me it was foolishness, and they deserved to be punished. That's what made them my favorites.

Oddly enough, Christians weren't all that hard to find in my world. Witches and warlocks threw house parties all the time, and often they would invite friends who claimed to be Christians—people who didn't know the secret lives we carried on apart from our jobs and daytime facades.

I strolled into just such a house party one night and scanned the room, reading the vibes that came off the people there and asking the spirits to direct me to the souls that were ripe for the plucking.

Julio, the man who hosted that night's party, flagged me down when I stepped through the front door. "Hey, John, you made it! Come on over here, man. I want to introduce you to someone."

I nodded back at him and headed in his direction, taking long, deliberate strides. I could see the guy he stood next to sizing me up, thinking, *Who is this tall man dressed all in black?*

I sensed a vibe of fascination…and maybe a little fear. Perfect. "What's happening?" I said as Julio and I shook hands. I darted my eyes to the stranger by his side.

"Oh, yeah," Julio said, "this is my friend Chris. He goes to church. You know, one of those holy rollers!" He jabbed Chris with his elbow and the guy laughed.

"How's it going, Chris?" I said politely, extending my hand. "My name is John." And then I stood back and watched the situation for a while, letting Julio and Chris banter on about nothing as the wine flowed and their tongues got looser. Every now and then I interjected something humorous into the conversation until Chris warmed up to me and regarded me as a new friend.

Excusing myself, I mingled throughout the party, renewing old acquaintances and making new ones. Sometime later that night I waited until the spirits told me it was time to invade Chris's spiritual space. I strolled over and refilled my wineglass next to where he was standing.

"Hey, Chris, we met earlier," I said. "Nice party going on. There's a few cute girls in here, huh?"

Chris smiled in recognition. "Oh, yeah...John, right? Yeah, dude, I know what you mean. I've been trying to chat up a few girls but no luck so far."

I ignored his comment and went in for the kill. "You know, there's something interesting that I know about you that the people in your life don't know."

Caught off guard, Chris laughed awkwardly. "Well, tell me, what do you know about me that nobody else knows? The suspense is killing me."

I kept a smile from spreading across my face. Without realizing it, his response had just opened a door for me to come into his spiritual space. I released a spirit of unbelief in his mind because I knew that the battlefield between him and me was in the mind. If I was able to capture a person's mind I was able to capture their heart, and that's how they became my victims no matter where I met them—lounges, subways, house gatherings.

I told him what had happened in his personal life that no one knew about, the skeletons hidden deep in his closet even though he claimed to be a Christian. I fought hard to keep a sneer off my face as I watched Chris's wide-eyed stare turn into a look of desperation and fear and, finally, helplessness. He was totally drained. It felt like I was choking him to death slowly, and I got a sense of power and enjoyment, ripping him open spiritually. I left him so dazed by my powers that he was already drunk in the spirit from the taste I had left behind.

Eager to prove my powers, I took every opportunity to show off the superiority of my religion, and sometimes that resulted in a battle of wills—and egos—between me and a good friend who was Muslim. We made light of it, but Muhammad and I taunted each other back and forth, him praising the powers of Allah and I declaring Satan the supreme ruler.

"I believe my religion is stronger than yours and I'm going to prove it to you," I said as we sauntered into the Step-In Diner in Parkchester late one afternoon and slid into a back booth. "Yours is a Mickey Mouse religion, and today's the day that you're going to have to prove it."

Muhammad glared at me with mock hostility. "Then I'll prove it."

We waited for the waitress to leave, and I leaned in across the table, pointing my finger in his direction. "Either your religion is bigger than mine, or mine is bigger than yours. You wanna see power? My religion and my daddy have more power than your religion. I'll give you the chance to go first."

I took a long drink of my soda and turned to the two girls sitting in the booth across from us. "Excuse me," I said to the dark-haired girl, "but my friend doesn't believe I have fortune-telling powers, and I want to prove it to him. He thinks he has them too. Would you allow us to tell you some things about your life?"

The girls looked at each other and giggled, then shrugged. "Why not?"

"I'm going to allow my friend Muhammad to go first," I said.

Muhammad turned to the girls. "You both got boyfriends, right? And you're both in love, right? And you've been with your boyfriends for a very long time."

The girls shook their heads and laughed. "You're way off," the dark-haired girl said. "Not true." She looked at me. "Now it's your turn."

Even as I prepared to speak I sensed the demon show up who was going to help me. I knew nothing about these girls—what walk of life they came from, what they were into—but I was about to read their mail in a way they never expected.

They thought it was a game, but instantly I turned serious. "You recently broke up with your boyfriend," I told the first girl. "You caught him cheating. This is the third time in your life that you've been stepped on by a man." Her face went blank and she looked across the booth at her friend in a wordless appeal.

"And you," I said, pointing to the other girl, "you're nothing but a spare tire. You're worthless. You hand yourself out to any man. You can't even get your own man. You don't even remember the last time you had a real relationship 'cause you're too busy taking other people's men."

The second girl's face turned red and her eyes pooled with tears, but I didn't care. I turned back to Mohammad and gave him a raised-eyebrow look.

"How do you know these things?" the dark-haired girl asked. Her friend was still too dumbfounded to speak.

I just laughed. "I told you—I have powers."

The girls tried to shake things off, not believing what had just happened, and they pointed in my direction. "He's the one with the powers. He's the powerful one."

That day Muhammad had to bow down to my god. His religion was worthless.

Too Far Gone

One night I went out and met up with a good friend in the religion, an NYPD narcotics officer who was also a warlock. We had already made up our minds which club to attend that night. He was out looking for girl-friends; I was looking for souls. I knew that night was a special night. *Zarabanda* and *Siete Rayos*, my two strongest spirits, were coming out with me, and they never disap-pointed. As we strolled down the sidewalk, I looked up at the sky. It was a clear spring night, and the heavens were crystal clear—you could count the stars in all that inky darkness, and the moon shone like the sun. I turned to Joe. "This is going to be a hell of a night. I feel it in the atmosphere."

He chuckled. "I'm ready for anything that comes our way, bro, especially some fine females."

I laughed in reply and smoothed my hand back over my jet-black hair. Dressed all in black, I knew I looked my best. As we entered the club, I heard the salsa music throbbing out its rhythmic beat. People whispered in the background as we walked in, and the smell of liquor hung heavy in the atmosphere. My mind was running at 90 miles an hour. Joe turned to me and smiled. "Wow, the place is packed with beautiful women, just the way I like it."

I smiled back.

We danced with the most beautiful women in the club, and I could sense the presence of the spirits looking around, trying to target someone I could speak to—someone I could do a reading with—but to my surprise there was no one there. I found that to be odd, but I kept dancing the night away with different women and making new friends. As the music wound down and the bartender yelled out "last call for alcohol" I went across the dance floor and told Joe it was time to go.

"Already?" he said in a drunken slur. "I'm just getting to know Wanda here."

"Now!" I snapped, not even looking at the girl. "Let's get out of here." Anger simmered in my chest at the night's failed mission.

To my surprise, when we stepped out of the club one of the spirits whispered, "Look to your right." There sat a panhandler in a wheelchair, begging for money outside the club. I fixed my eyes on him and went straight at him, knowing he was going to be my prey for the night. I was half demon-possessed when I got up to where he sat—no longer me.

"Do you want to make a bet?" I said, a sneer spreading across my face.

Surprised, the panhandler remained silent and glanced from me to Joe to see what was up.

"Hey, come on, bro, leave him alone," Joe said, nudging me with his arm.

I shook him off and glared at the man in the wheelchair. "I said do you want to make a bet? I'm willing to bet the money I have left in my pocket to the money you have in that pathetic paper cup. That's a whole night's take, isn't it?" I added with a sinister grin.

"What are we betting on?" the panhandler asked.

My smile froze. "Your life."

He gave a nervous laugh. "The bet is on."

"Good," I said. "I can tell you your whole life story in ten minutes and how you ended up in that wheelchair. Are you up for the challenge?"

The man shrugged. "I got nothing to lose."

"Only your soul," I murmured. "Tonight's your lucky night." As I went on to describe his life, I could see that I was breaking him bit by bit spiritually. What started with a chuckle and a smile ended up in tears and sorrow. I knew I had him just where I wanted him—to the point that I tried to force him off the chair and make him walk, even though he was paralyzed.

"Stand up, you lousy beggar! Stand up and face me down like a man!" I shouted.

The panhandler crumpled over in his wheelchair and covered his face with his hands, his sobs escaping into the now-silent night.

Joe stood by with a blank look on his face. I knew that as soon as I was done with this man he was destined for hell. As I won the bet and left him sobbing in a pool of tears, I took his cup full of change and threw it into the street.

Before I turned to leave, I leaned over the man and said in a low voice, "You're a waste of a life on Planet Earth. Nobody loves you. Why don't you do yourself a favor and die?"

"Now it's time to go," I said to Joe, jerking my head in the direction we should walk. I could hear his voice cracking as he tried to speak up, like he had a knot in his throat. All that came out was "John, John…"

I looked up and saw tears in Joe's eyes.

"What's the matter?" I spat out. "You can't handle it? Aren't you a devil worshipper as well as I am?"

He just stood there, shaking his head. "John, I can't hang with you no more, man. You're too far gone."

That night I knew I had reached a place in my walk with the devil that left many others behind who were in the same occult inner circle. As we made it to Joe's building, I sensed he had reached a breaking point. It didn't matter that he was a police officer, seeing so many harsh things in the world we live in. What he saw tonight pushed him beyond his limit.

I turned to him for the last time. "You're nothing but a disappointment to the religion. I thought you wanted to move up the ranks, but you have no heart for the spirits. Go to hell and goodnight."

As I walked away, strolling down the avenue toward my own home, I felt fearless—like I could take on the world. The streetlamps overhead illuminated the sidewalk with a silvery light. As I crossed the streets I felt the familiar predator instinct churn in my gut. I looked around to see if anyone was out on the avenue that I could prey on, but the streets were as empty as the cemetery I hung out in from time to time.

Hitting Rock Bottom

The months went by and turned into years as I dedicated my every waking moment to pleasing Satan and the spirit gods of my religion. But I missed my daughter Amanda so much it hurt. I felt spiritually exhausted from lending my body out to demonic forces, hunting for victims in clubs, and feeling the weight of loss from Amanda's increasing absence in my life. The older she grew, the less time she had for me.

One morning I got up and something just clicked in my brain, like flipping a switch. "I'm not doing this anymore," I said out loud to the four walls. "I don't even care if I die." For death was a near certainty. Anyone who tried to leave the religion faced a death penalty and soon became the victim of some freak accident or sudden illness. I'd seen it happen several times.

As I began to be disobedient to the demons' requests everything in my world fell apart. I no longer did the rituals and stopped showing up for certain witchcraft meetings. As I started to lose power, my life careened into a two-year living hell on earth. In the long painful process of my divorce, I lost a $40,000-a-year job with a shipping company. No one knew of my woes because I kept my life private. I knew how to deceive people into thinking things were going well with me. But the truth was, with no employment and no money I ended up homeless, living in the first-floor vacant apartment I had been evicted from. Every night I climbed through the window just to stay off the streets.

During the day I roamed around like a zombie walking the earth, not having a clue or sense of direction. Mine was a life of broken pieces, and I had no idea when it would come together. As the daylight waned and darkness stole over the earth, I pretended I was the man I used to be—always having somewhere to go, something to do, people to see. I would roam until late at night, walking the streets of Castle Hill in an aimless rhythm. Every corner I turned showed nothing but concrete sidewalks and concrete buildings, with the smell of death in the air. I wondered how much time I had left here on earth.

As I approached my old apartment building, I looked around to make sure no one followed me home before turning the corner into the dead-end street the apartment faced. I acted like I was looking for something on the ground, then jumped up, opened the front window slightly, and dropped into the empty, dark apartment that

I called home. Curling up on the bare floor, with no heat to stave off the freezing cold, I fell into a fitful sleep.

But oftentimes sleep eluded me and I would stare at the empty apartment that once had been filled with life. In my mind, I could hear the laughter of my daughter as she ran around the apartment. I envisioned her playing in the center of the room with all her toys and dolls. I could hear her calling my name, "Daddy, Daddy!" When I eventually fell asleep, I would awaken in the middle of the night hoping she would be there so I could hold her and kiss her, letting her know how much I loved her. But instead of Amanda's little-girl giggle, all I could hear now was the sound of rats running across the living room floor. This was my reality, and I could not wake up from it.

I cried myself to sleep on the cold hard floor surrounded by darkness—a cruel reminder of what my life had become, dark with no light. Where had I gone wrong? Life had no meaning anymore. All this went on until I landed on public assistance, and eventually I found an affordable apartment on McGraw Avenue across the street from my mother's building.

Stolen Sight

Because I didn't return to the religion fully, a deeper punishment came—a curse that harkened back to my childhood initiation into Santeria. *"Your son is on the verge of losing his sight..."* I remembered Cookie telling my mother when I was just ten years old. Now the old curse had come to claim me because of my disobedience to the spirits. Out of the clear blue the retinas of both eyes began to detach. To correct this, I had one operation after the other—a total of seven—but to no avail. I was completely blind. It is one thing to be born blind but quite another to lose your sight after seeing the sky, the birds, the faces of family, friends, and even those you hate.

What had life done to me now? After thirty years of seeing everything I wanted to see, now I couldn't even see my own hand in front of my face. Was God punishing me? Or testing me? Why would I be able to see for thirty years and suddenly not see at all? Each blind person's experience is unique. For me, it was like a grayish mist came down over my vision, or like a cloudy day sitting on top of my eyes. What an experience. I learned to depend on my hearing and touching through my hands.

The funniest things, the small things that didn't matter, or the things you never took notice of, you suddenly crave when you're blind, and those thoughts constantly run through your mind. Life is gray and not by choice. It's like a whole different dimension where your world closes in. It's like living in your world with no visitors. What was important at one time doesn't matter anymore. Emptiness and sorrow become your friends.

The doctors told me I had two choices: a seeing-eye dog or a cane to maneuver myself around with.

That's when my mother decided it was time for me to move back closer to her. By now I lived on the twelfth floor in her building and she lived on the second. But with the new arrangement, I stayed in her apartment. She knew about the crazy religion I had been involved in, but she wasn't afraid of my demons. I was her son, and she was going to take good care of me.

My world came to a stop. Losing it all, losing my vision, I lay in one of the back rooms of her apartment, with a treatment of eye drops every four hours. From somewhere in the apartment I could hear a clock ticking, counting off the seconds of my new life—seconds that seemed to stretch into an eternity of nothingness. Doctor's orders required that I lie twelve hours in bed on my back and twelve hours on my stomach after squeezing the prescription drops into my eyes: twelve hours face-up and twelve hours face-down. The only time I was allowed to get up was to go to the bathroom, shower, or eat. This regimen went on for six months—I was unable to sit up, unable to go outside. It took a toll on me mentally, and as I lay in bed I recapped the good times I spent in the clubs.

"Mom!" I would yell out from my bed. "What time is it?"

And she would answer back, calling out the time. If it was 11:30 p.m., I would recall dancing the night away with beautiful women, or drawing a soul into my dark religion through a reading in a smoke-filled room. Remembering the past and how I went about my daily and nightly activities kept my mind from cracking.

At my next appointment two weeks later, the doctor took me into an examination room and looked into the retina of my right eye. My vision wasn't getting any better, which meant it was time for drastic measures.

The doctor turned to me and whispered, "Today we're going to do a procedure that will be one of the most difficult you ever experience. We will not use anesthesia for this one."

As he got up, I looked the doctor straight in his eyes and said, "Do whatever you have to do, it's fine with me," not realizing what was about to take place.

The doctor reached out for one of the longest needles I had ever seen. The thing must have been about six or seven inches long. As he came back and sat down, he said to me, "You must be still and grip the chair with both of your hands and look toward me. Don't even blink your eye. I'm going to insert this needle straight into your pupil so it can hit the back of your eye behind the retina and form an air pocket. That will allow your retina to heal faster."

When he stuck the needle through my eye, I gripped the chair with all my might and felt my blood run cold. I was not able to move or blink as he kept pushing the needle deeper into my eye.

But no matter what the doctors did, the disappointment in my mother's voice painted a picture I didn't want to see. I would be this way for a long time to come.

During my follow-up appointment I got more bad news. I already knew I had low vision, but now the doctor used a term that made my stomach feel like a bag full of rocks—legally blind.

In late fall of that year, I met with a counselor from the Commission of the Blind for my interview, and my case was accepted. From there, I was evaluated and placed into a program tailor-made just for me while counselors monitored my progress. I would learn to do all the things blind people do in order to survive.

One morning after almost a year without normal vision, I got up and felt something strange in my eyes. A tiny bit of light shone through.

"Mom, come quick!" I called from the back room of the apartment.

"What is it, John," my mother said as she came through the door.

I held up my hand and waved it back and forth in front of my eyes. A glimmer of light from the window created enough illumination for me to see the movement, slight though it was.

"John, are you saying…" Her words dropped off, and her voice caught in her throat.

"I can see."

I was allowed to go out regularly under supervision, and in time my vision returned fully. I shared my experience with members of the religion, and soon after I returned to witchcraft with a new devotion. How I thanked my fellow witches and warlocks for praying for me, and for all the spirits for helping me in my time of need. My gratefulness propelled me full force into the dark side, serving the devil and casting spells on those who got in my way. I also remained faithful in luring new recruits from bars, clubs, lounges—wherever I could find them. I would prey on people by telling them their fortune and then destroy them.

A Flying Demon

Now that I was rededicated to the demon world, the spirits gave me a new assignment—and the power and ability to go with it. At night as I slept, I was able to leave my body and fly over neighborhoods, hurling taunts and curses down on the people who lived within their borders. Caught in the grip of strange dreams, I would catch myself being transported into different neighborhoods within the five boroughs of New York City. These out-of-body experiences allowed me to have dominion over the communities. I felt diabolical, devilish, like a vampire, and knew they had nothing on me. Sometimes I would even land and walk around the neighborhoods, bringing curses, bad luck, and the witchcraft aura.

Oddly, however, in some neighborhoods I met with strong resistance and at first couldn't understand where the opposing power came from. In these neighborhoods, people were waiting for me to land. I prepared to curse the neighborhood, but when I landed a mob would chase me for blocks and I couldn't curse them. Frustrated, I would fly off again, hovering as high as the streetlamps, and they would look up at me. Finally I realized these were the nasty Christians praying for their neighborhoods, their communities, their families—the prayers of the people I hated the most. Wherever these praying Christians lived, I couldn't penetrate the neighborhood. I got in, but I couldn't do the evil acts I had come to perform. So I would move on to the next neighborhood. This was my calling, and it was also what I loved to do.

Chapter 9

Selling My Soul to the Devil

The afternoon I learned about Palo Mayombe in Aunt Maria's basement—the same day I met New York City's highest-ranked godfather in the religion—was a turning point for me. I knew I was going to a level in the spirit realm that others only dreamed about. In Palo Mayombe, you're dealing straight with the devil. You learn to make evil spirits do your bidding. By the time I left Aunt Maria's house it was dark outside, and I was excited as I stepped through the gate to head home. I knew I had to get the money together to do the initiation ceremony— it would cost me $3500 to become a Palero, a priest for the dark side, but I already considered it money well spent.

A few days later we all met up at my aunt's house, and the high *tata* priest told those who were chosen to become priests of Palo Mayombe the do's and don'ts of the final ceremony—what procedures would take place, what time to be there, what to wear—but first would come a ritual performed in the mountains at night. I glanced around the room. Along with me, sixteen other men stood ready to make a contract with the devil. The *tata* told us that once you start the journey toward becoming a Palero, you can't turn back. The spirits exact a death sentence on any cowards who don't complete the ritual.

A guy across the room caught my eye and quickly looked away. I could see fear stamped on his face; another one looked vaguely puzzled, not knowing whether to say yes or no, but we all knew that saying no would not only be a death sentence, it would make us an embarrassment to the religion. The room throbbed with fear and excitement. We were stepping into something unknown, walking into this black hole called Palo Mayombe.

Ritual in the Mountains

Two weeks later we met at a location in the Bronx and drove up into the hills, arriving there at five o'clock in the evening. It was already dusk when I got out of my car. We gathered together in a circle with the godfather, and I could tell by his eyes that he was already half demon-possessed. He wore the same familiar bandana I remembered from the day I first met him in Aunt Maria's basement. No one spoke. We waited to take our cues from him.

The *tata* tilted his head back and half-closed his eyes. "*Mi padre* [my father], this is your son," he intoned in a singsong voice. "I'm coming into the mountain, I'm coming into your house. I'm asking permission to come into your presence. I love you, I love you, I love you. This is your son...receive this ceremony and the offering I bring..."

As he chanted, he gripped a bottle of white rum in one hand and a cigar in the other. Turning to head up the mountain, he led the way blowing cigar smoke, spraying rum, and tossing twenty-one pennies as a gesture of respect to the spirits waiting for us up in the hills—*Zarabanda, Siete Rayos,* and *Madre Agua.* We fell in line behind him, echoing his words like a chorus. A few other people lingered in the playground area and parking lot, eyeing us strangely, but we didn't care—we were bold and fearless, and they stared wide-eyed as the high priest led the way chanting songs to the spirits. A second priest gripped a giant machete in his hand, holding it up as we climbed the mountain.

The dark evergreens and leafless oaks stood out like black silhouettes at the top of the mountain, and the bone-chilling cold cut through me. I watched as the high priest approached a specific tree in the woods. He sprayed it with rum from his mouth, then blew cigar smoke and placed the machete on the ground in front of the tree. On each side of the blade he drew a straight line with symbols of skulls and crosses. He turned his back to the tree out of respect for the spirits and lit up the machete with gunpowder. A puff of black smoke appeared. Somebody gasped at the small explosion. I fought the urge to see who it was, knowing the ritual demanded my full respect and attention.

"You two come forward, and the rest stay behind," the *tata* said, his eyes boring into mine. He gestured for me and Aunt Maria to go first. Two by two we came to the tree, rolled up our pants above the knees, removed our shoes and socks, and kneeled on the frozen ground. As a male, I had to remove my shirt, and we both placed our hands up against the tree while the *tata* sprayed rum and blew cigar smoke on us, chanting a strange language.

We could not move or open our eyes for about fifteen minutes—an eternity of time when the temperature is near zero. It was so cold the palms of my hands stuck to the tree from the frost, and I shook like a leaf. But I wasn't about to turn back. I was fascinated, not fearful. The tangible power in the wooded clearing was indescribable.

After each of the initiates completed their ritual, we headed back down the mountain. As the godfather walked along he sang, and once again we repeated the chants. At the bottom of the mountain, the people still hanging out stared at us as if they had seen a ghost. The irony hit me and I laughed to myself. *Not a ghost but something a lot more powerful.* We got in our cars and left.

Losing My Soul

The final part of the priesthood ceremony took place a week later in Aunt Maria's basement. We weren't allowed to eat from noon onward that day, and the ceremony started at 6 p.m. Excitement pulsed in my veins. By midnight that evening I would belong to Satan, and I would bear the marks on my body to prove it. As I approached the house on foot, I could feel the rhythm of the conga drums vibrating on the night air. The sound of chanting inside told me that those who came to watch the ceremony—seasoned priests of the religion—were beckoning the spirits, setting the spiritual atmosphere for what would take place that night.

The morning after the ceremony, I stepped quietly into the bathroom, leaned into the mirror, and looked at my reflection. My dark eyes glowed with an inner fire that spoke of the contract I had made the night before. The cross-shaped cut on my forehead still oozed, raw and bloody, and the various other cuts on my body stung the way untreated wounds always do—especially after a night of sleeping on a cold concrete floor. I changed into a clean set of clothes, all white, and put on a baseball cap to cover the wound on my forehead. Not wanting to wake the other initiates, who were still asleep on the basement floor, I slipped out the door as silent as a mouse and headed for the nearest diner.

The diner bustled with early-morning business, and as I stood in line at the counter I thought back to everything that had happened the night before.

"Next...can I help you?" the counter clerk said.

I turned my eyes toward the woman and she recoiled. Instantly I knew she could sense the evil in me.

"I'll have a chocolate donut and a hot chocolate," I said, my eyes boring into hers.

The woman's hand trembled as she rang up my order. "Are you all right?" she asked in a timid voice.

I lifted up my hat and showed her the cross carved into my flesh. "I just sold my soul to the devil last night."

She went pale. "Oh, my God!"

"Anything else you want to know? Just give me my donut!" I threw my money on the counter and waited for the order to come up. As I waited, I felt a presence of something else in the diner, something I couldn't put my finger on. I turned to look down the length of booths that lined the wall of the diner. Nothing but customers—regular people out for breakfast and their daily caffeine fix. Years later I learned that a woman sitting at a back booth with a friend saw me dressed all in white and knew that I was a *Palero Tata*. Unbeknownst to me, she lifted her hands in prayer that day, and her prayers were for me.

Demons on Assignment

My pact with the devil only caused me to step up the clubbing scene. I stepped into bars and clubs and lounges so often they seemed more familiar than my own home. The taste of wine and the sound of jazz and salsa music blended into a never-ending haze of casting spells by day and recruiting souls by night.

There was a lounge in my neighborhood where all the pretty people loved to go, and one Tuesday night I got myself ready and headed out alone because at this point almost no one in the religion wanted to hang with me— like Joe, they thought I was too far gone. It was a world of jealousy, a love/hate religion, and people would not hang out with you if they thought you were more powerful than they were. Even the bartenders dreaded to see me come in, knowing I would steal all the pretty women at the bar. I could read it in their eyes: *We don't have a chance now that you're here.*

A big bouncer collected admission fees at the door to the bar. When he looked at me, fear gripped him and he waved me inside. "Go away, man. Gone on…don't worry about it."

"Cool," I said, and started to go inside.

"Wait a minute," the bouncer said. He threw some chips in my hand to buy free drinks with. As I made my way to the bar, I said hello to a few people I knew, got a seat at the corner of the bar, and looked across to the opposite side. There sat Carlos, an NYPD officer who was also in the religion, so I went over and we started shooting the breeze.

Deep into the night a girl named Jennifer, one of my favorite young ladies, made her way from downtown to the Bronx to hang out with me. After she located me at the bar, I introduced her to Carlos and we all started talking and laughing. Jennifer was the type who liked to roam around the place to get attention. Beautiful from head to toe, with light brown eyes, she grabbed everyone's attention as soon as she came in. As she paraded herself through the bar, tossing her long black hair, my friend and I kept talking about the religion and his police work.

"Hey, John," Carlos said sometime later, nudging me. "Your date's over there entertaining two guys at the bar."

I glanced in the direction he indicated and shrugged.

"Are you planning to do something about it? 'Cause if so I've got your back."

I swallowed a mouthful of wine and set the glass on the counter. "She's nothing but a piece of furniture, Carlos. Don't worry about it. By the end of the night I guarantee you she'll be back by my side."

Suddenly I had an idea. "You want to see how strong my demonic powers are?" I asked Carlos. He nodded, so I called to the bartender and told him to give me a white napkin and a pen. I drew symbols of Palo Mayombe on the napkin to call upon demonic spirits to show up at the bar and confuse the atmosphere. As that took place, *Siete Rayos* showed up. I could feel his presence in the bar. I knew that night the bar was never going to be the same. The place heated up like it was on fire, and people seemed very uneasy, not understanding what was going on.

As the night drew to a close, Jennifer jumped off her stool across the bar and made her way to me, wrapping her arms around my back. The two guys she'd been partying with strolled over in my direction, and I looked at them and smiled. I pointed my finger at them. "You're police officers," I said, and they froze in their tracks because they were undercover cops, not uniformed policemen.

"See?" I said. "She's leaving with me, but you two will learn a lesson tonight that you will never forget, not because of her—she means nothing to me."

The two men looked confused. "What are you talking about, man? What are you trying to say?"

I stared them down. "You know what I'm talking about...you're police officers, and I'm going to teach you a lesson about respecting people. You will know that this night you messed with the devil." I turned around and left the bar with Jennifer.

Three weeks later I was bored at home and decided to make my way to the lounge in my neighborhood. As I took a seat at the bar, Louie the bartender approached me and said, "What's up? How you been?"

"Nothing new," I answered. "Just the same old, same old. I just wanted to come out and hear some jazz and have a nice chill glass of wine."

"Anything for you, John," he said.

As I sat at the bar, a few minutes later Lou came over and leaned down close.

"There're two gentlemen across the bar, and they're afraid of approaching you, but they want to know if they can buy you a drink."

I looked across the bar and recognized the two guys I had encountered three weeks ago, the ones who had partied with Jennifer.

"Lou, they don't have to buy me a drink," I said. "I got my own money. Who are they to think they can buy me a drink? If they want to come over and talk to me, so be it." As the two men came over, they wore a look of respect and fear on their faces.

"Can we talk to you for a few minutes?" they said. "My name is Rick, and this is my partner Tony."

"What can I do for you?" I said.

The guy named Rick spoke first. "We've been coming here for three weeks looking for you. We wanted to tell you we're sorry for what happened that night with the girl. We stayed away from her; we haven't called her. We wanted you to know that something we could never imagine happened to us in our apartment. We just want to call peace with you, so whatever you sent to our apartment, you can remove it."

I was laughing inside. I knew what had happened, but I acted like an innocent little boy, waiting to hear the full story of what took place that night.

Rick glanced at Tony and started talking first. "When we got home that evening, we decided to call it a night and headed for our rooms. Sometime that night after we fell asleep we heard noises in the living room and kitchen—like a person was walking around the apartment. It was crazy, man. We both were feeling the same thing, but we were in two different rooms. Dishes rattled, heavy steps thudded through the living room, and the apartment went ice cold. Paralyzed with fear, we finally reached for our guns and got up. As we headed to the living room, the sound got louder, and when Tony and I came into the room we heard maniacal laughter—even though we could see that nothing was there."

Rick turned and looked at his friend Tony. "Right, Tony? Isn't that what happened?"

"Look at my pendant of *San Lazaro*," Tony said. "It got twisted like a pretzel. We wanted to run out of the house, and we stayed up all night, unable to sleep. This went on for a few nights in a row. That's when we decided to come to the bar and call it peace. We wanted to apologize for any misunderstanding. Are we cool?"

"The next time you disrespect me in any way, I'll be going to your funeral," I said, sipping my wine nonchalantly. "I will withdraw the demon that I sent over to your house, but don't let it happen again."

From that night on we became good friends.

Warlock for Hire

Casting spells is not just what warlocks "do"—it's what they do for money, and if you're good the opportunities can be lucrative. Anyone looking for a shortcut to success, or influence with the right people, or a witchcraft "hit man" to take somebody out would call on me. If the price was right and the job appealed to me, I took it. One day I ran into a friend of mine named Big John. Big asked me for help in finding him a job because he knew how strong my powers were. I was the real thing, a *Palero Tata*, and you couldn't get any higher in the occult. Naturally the spell worked: Big landed the job of his dreams, but at a price—his life would be indebted to the demonic spirits that now controlled his life.

Big and I had a lot in common: fast cars, beautiful women, smooth liquor, and noisy clubs. Every once in a while when I went to the club in my neighborhood, I would run into him. The next time I saw Big he approached me about a favor for a friend, a young girl named Courtney who was in trouble. He kept pestering me to help this girl, and each time he did I told him no. But he persisted, saying she would pay me a lot of money for my services.

I laughed at him. "Do I look like I need money?"

I managed to stay away from Big John for a while because I really didn't want to help this Courtney girl. But two months later I ran into him again with the same request. I was sick of hearing it, so I attended a demonic feast where many mediums were possessed, and there I took the opportunity to ask for advice. I asked a demon spirit what he thought about me helping Courtney. The spirit told me not to hold back on her or anyone else who wanted help because it would make all the demons in my life happy. A few days later I caught up with Big John and told him I would help his lady friend.

He gave me Courtney's number, so I called her up at work and arranged for her to have a reading done at my place. "Come to my house with Big John at 8 p.m.," I said. Since I was dealing with a total stranger, I had to know first what kind of favor she wanted and why.

The night of the reading, Big showed up at my door with Courtney. I ushered them into the living room, and Courtney handed me a large paper bag. I opened it to inspect what was inside. Good. Everything I had instructed her to bring was there: the candles, the liquor, along with twenty-one dollars and twenty-one cents. I told them to sit and relax while I fetched some cold soda from the kitchen. While they waited, I went into my closet, closed the door, and chanted over the cauldron, blowing cigar smoke into the cast-iron pot until two high-ranking demons showed up. The cauldron, or Jewel, is a cast-iron pot weighing over a hundred pounds with the devil's face engraved on it. It is an important part of witchcraft, a place to meet with the devil and his demons, a place of pure evil that grips you with fear from head to toe. It is the devil-spot where the supernatural meets the natural to induce powers beyond human comprehension and evil that can be felt and touched. You can use it to kill, steal, and destroy those who get in your way. I was a hit man in the supernatural who could take out you and your family or anyone else I was hired to destroy. How can you stop something this evil and unseen when it is sent to attack you and destroy your life? That is the purpose of the cauldron, and I was one of the best at using this demonic tool to accomplish hell on earth.

I could feel the demons' presence and I knew who they were. They introduced themselves in my spirit. A few minutes later I was transformed into someone other than me, possessed with one of the demons. Although possessed, I was very conscious of what needed to be accomplished. Now it was time to begin Courtney's reading. But everything had to go right. It was a very sacred moment.

Back in the living room, Courtney sat across from me at the table. Everything was set. Now would come the interrogation.

"Whatever I ask, I want you to answer yes or no. No explanations or stories. Understand?" That was the first question I threw at her. It was a test.

"Yes," she said.

I looked her straight in the eye and asked her the next question.

"I know that you came from a broken home, and you've been abused. Yes or no?"

"Yes."

So far she was telling the truth.

"You also have a boyfriend, and he's physically abused you. And you had two abortions and one miscarriage." Her answer had to be yes.

"Yes."

As the reading went on, the demonic symbols I had drawn on the floor prior to the reading looked as if they were on fire.

"I know you were fired from your job."

"Yes," she said.

"A sneaker store?"

"Yes."

"I know you stole from there."

Courtney went silent.

"No…no…"

The demons told me to stop the reading.

I banged my first on the table. "You're a liar! Get out, and don't you ever come back." Courtney began crying out loud.

Big John looked shocked at what took place. I answered before he could even ask the question. "This piece of trash was trying to deceive me."

Courtney spoke up. "The reason I lied was because I wanted to find out if you were the real thing."

"You want to see the real thing?" I said. "Okay, I'll prove it. You stole $20,000 from your boss, and he's taking you to court to put you in jail."

Courtney started crying again. "It was my boyfriend. He said he'd leave me if I didn't take care of him."

"You're supporting this low-life, aren't you?" I asked her. She didn't have to tell me how every man who had come into her life treated her the same way.

"I've been to plenty of tarot readers," Courtney said. "All phonies. But never have I met anyone like you."

I told Courtney to leave because I didn't deal with liars. But she pleaded with me to help her get out of trouble. That's when a demon whispered to me: *Tell her on the next visit, she can make a contract with us.*

Four nights later she came over to my place with Big John as witness to initiate the witchcraft ritual. She brought all the ingredients, a recipe from hell to destroy her enemies who were accusing her. This was to be a very serious meeting. Foolishness was punishable by death.

Courtney agreed to do whatever the demons wanted. If she was convicted in a court of law, she would face five years in prison and a $20,000 fine to make up for her employer's losses in stolen cash and merchandise. The demons promised that if she kept her end of the contract, there was no need to worry.

The first step to Courtney's acquittal required a spiritual cleansing. This was not an initiation ceremony to induct her into the religion but rather a ritual used to get people out of situations they were guilty of. The atmosphere was thick. Even the roosters felt the fear of what was going to happen next—they were about to be beheaded, their feet hacked off, and their blood poured into the prepared cauldron as an offering to strengthen the agreement in Courtney's contract for an acquittal.

As Big and Courtney were leaving the apartment, I assured her that her accusers would experience hell itself. I was going to punish them like they'd never been punished before. Three days later, Courtney went to court. That morning the judge was in a foul mood. The top prosecutor would be coming in late. Actually, he wouldn't be coming in at all. A bad car accident had landed him in the hospital, and he was the stand-in for the first attorney, who had mysteriously gotten ill. Now a pair of backup lawyers would have to take the place of the one hospitalized. And as soon as they arrived, the circus began. They just couldn't get their facts together, and because of that they disagreed with each other, and they were on the same team.

Toward the end of the grueling trial, when the frustrated judge shouted at both opposing lawyers for arguing with him and for babbling confusing nonsense, he finally summoned the jurors into the jury room to deliberate.

A short time later, everyone shuffled out of the room and back to the jury box. They had reached a decision.

With the slam of the gavel, the judge made the announcement: The case was dropped and all charges against Courtney were dismissed. Although the defending lawyer wore a big smile, I wore a bigger one. How easily deceived they all were. That day, Courtney and I thought we were winners.

With the trial over, Courtney eventually became my goddaughter in the religion and resumed her life. But she would never get to enjoy it. Now that she had been introduced to witchcraft, there was a price to pay. Her life was no longer hers, to do with as she wanted. She belonged to the demons she had dared to seek help from. Although Courtney never spent a day in jail for what she did, her real prison sentence was just beginning. She would be a victim, owned by the spirits of *espiritismo*, Santeria, and Palo Mayombe for life.

Chapter 10

Rachael – The Prodigal Encounter

I rolled over in bed and squinted at the clock on my nightstand—it was past noon. I groaned, not just at the late hour but at the throbbing in my head. The previous night of clubbing and drinking was to blame. If I didn't take a shower now and get dressed, I would never finish all the errands I needed to take care of for that day, and it was a long ride by train to 42nd Street. How I missed my sports car.

A block later, I pushed through the turnstile of the downtown Six Train on Parkchester when all of a sudden I saw this beautiful young lady walk right past me. Dressed all in black, she had long dark hair, pale skin, and wore a pair of stiletto heels as she cat-walked by me. Suddenly I no longer wanted to do errands. I had a date. The only thing was, this young woman in the dazzling black outfit didn't know it was her. I walked toward her—masquerading the obvious—and stood a gentleman's distance away. A moment later, the train pulled into the station with a rush of air and jerked to a stop. I looked at my watch with one eye, and with the other I glanced to see which compartment she went into.

On hurried steps I followed closed behind her. That was when the doors decided to close on me, but with quick hands I squeezed my way through. She took a seat and I sat facing her. What long, gorgeous black hair she had. She was my kind of girl. I wondered why she was alone—unless she was on her way to meet someone. I had to find out. I let a few train stops go by in order to practice my lines, then waited until her eyes met mine.

"By the way are you into modeling?" I asked.

She smiled and looked away.

I tried again.

"Excuse me, miss. That's a lovely dress you're wearing. Black is my favorite color. Where are you going dressed like that?"

Finally she spoke. "School."

"Really? Where?"

"Baruch College."

"So what are you majoring in?"

"Business."

The train was swallowed up by the long, dark tunnel, making a lot of noise.

"Mind if I sit next to you? That way I can hear you better."

With her eyes she invited me to the empty seat beside her, and I took it gladly.

"I don't mean to be nosey, but do you live in the area where you boarded?"

"Yes. Lived there for nineteen years."

"I've been there for fifteen. How come I've never seen you?"

"Our paths have never crossed."

When the train pulled into the 125th Street station, we switched for the waiting downtown Four Express.

The train rumbled fast into the dark tunnel, and I asked her another question.

"Where are you from?"

"I was born and raised in the Bronx," she said.

"Yeah? Me too. Only I was born in PR, then I moved here." I couldn't stop talking to her. "What kind of work do you do?"

"I'm a manager in a cosmetics store."

"Hip. Where?"

"Forty-ninth Street and Third Avenue." She studied me, and I realized what she was about to ask. "So what do you do with your life?"

I couldn't tell her I was a devil worshipper. "I freelance installing artwork in galleries and showrooms."

With the train rushing over the tracks, bypassing local stations and waiting straphangers with a blur, the conversation turned personal. I didn't ask her to tell me she loved traveling, Broadway shows, and dining out or that after schoolwork was done, she enjoyed watching romantic movies and reading novels. But she did.

"So what are your interests?" she said.

I would have to give her an edited version of my life, leaving out the wild parties, the clubbing, carousing with beautiful women, and that other thing I did.

"I like the same things you do," I told her in a nutshell.

She told me she had a two-year-old daughter named Sarah. So I told her I had a daughter too. "Her name is Amanda."

The train pulled into Grand Central Station, but I decided not to get off at my stop. I wanted to continue on and keep her company. We both got off at Union Square, and together we walked out to the street. I thanked her for the talk and kissed her on the cheek. "Hope I run into you again." I knew I would, because right there she gave me her phone number on a piece of paper. I read it. Her name was Rachael.

I let a few days go by without calling Rachael. What was the rush? I had more important things to take care of, like buying a new luxury car. I had to impress the other ladies I was dating, so with the money I was making at my current job, and money I made in witchcraft, I treated myself.

A week later, I called Rachael at her workplace.

"How are things going?" I asked.

"Fine."

"Listen, I have a surprise for you. How long are you going to be there?"

She told me her schedule. She would be there till 7 p.m. Since I was in the area I had plenty of time to stop by a florist and pick up a dozen white roses. When I got to 49th and Third Avenue, I parked my car, crossed the street, and entered the fancy cosmetic store. I surprised her with the flowers and she surprised me with a kiss. She seemed happy to see me.

I handed her the card that came with the roses and we talked for a few minutes. Inside the card, I had written my phone number along with a romantic message, and as soon as she opened it an uneasy feeling swept over me. That was when the voice of a demon interrupted: "You must leave right away."

If I left as commanded, I would lose the opportunity for the moment that was building. I ignored the warning. But it hammered in my head again: "Don't make me repeat myself. Leave now!"

"Listen," I said. "I gotta go. We'll meet some other time."

She begged me to stay, but despite her sweet pleading, I left in a hurry and went straight home. Sometime later I checked my phone for voice mail, and when I did the strange message blared through: "You'd better stay away from Rachael. You hear? I'm the father of her daughter."

I was dumbfounded. I had no idea she and the baby's father were still together. Rachael had told me she was a single mother who had put off dating. I had to hear her side of the story before making a judgment call.

Her father, Robert, was the one who picked up the phone. I told him who I was and he put Rachael on.

"Hi, John. What a surprise."

"Rachael, I got to tell you about something that happened." I told her the story about the message left by her charming boyfriend.

"Right after you left the cosmetic store that day, he came in," she said, apologizing. No wonder the demon told me to leave. He knew there was trouble coming. I listened to the rest of what Rachael had to say. "As soon as my ex-boyfriend entered the store and saw the roses, he went ballistic. He ripped the petals off the flowers, grabbed the card out of my hands, and blistered about some important business he had to take care of. That's how he got your number. He also threatened me."

"What'd he say?" I asked.

"That if I continued seeing you, he would make hell out of my life."

I had to know the truth. "Do you still love him?"

"No," she responded. "I don't want to see him anymore. It's all over between us."

I could tell by Rachael's tone that she was telling the truth. I sighed out my relief. "Listen, would you like to go out for dinner sometime soon? I know this great restaurant downtown you'd really like."

She accepted. But before we went out on our first date, I needed to get more information on her ex-boyfriend. But not from Rachael. At that time I knew I could summon a demon and he would tell me everything I wanted to know. I took a coconut, smashed it, and got the broken pieces ready for the reading into Rachael's ex. I threw the fragmented coconut shells into the air, and the way they landed on the floor—the number of curved pieces facing up versus those facing down—would determine the kind of questions I was allowed to ask. I stood in front of the cauldron to get my answers. I blew cigar smoke, sprayed white rum, and took the coconut shells to get my questions answered. The demons told me everything I needed to know about Rachael's ex-boyfriend. I knew he was dangerous and diabolical, and I knew I had to destroy him—kill him with witchcraft.

It was the day of my first date with Rachael. I waited in front of her parents' building, and when she came out she was as lovely as the day I saw her on the train.

The trip from the Bronx to Manhattan was smooth. Traffic on the FDR was moderate and the weather was just right. Romance was in the air; Rachael fell in love with my new car at first sight.

We walked into a quiet Italian restaurant on 83rd on the west side of Manhattan, and right away she loved the rustic ambiance of another culture. She told me stories that made me laugh; I told ones that almost made her cry.

With the evening still young, Rachael and I decided to go for a stroll. The night was crisp, the moon was out, and as we passed trendy dress shops and boutiques, we held hands. Rachael and I were off to a flying start, and we both knew it.

On the way back to the car, the silence we shared was better than anything said. Now it was back to the Bronx. I let salsa music pulsate through the stereo speakers while listening to Rachael's voice. She was such a great gabber. I loved the way she laughed, and she loved the way I drove. With each moment that passed I got to know her better, and she became more acquainted with me—but only what I chose to reveal to her.

The drive home came to an end and I pulled up to her building. What would a gentleman do in this situation, I asked myself. We were alone in the car and she seemed not to mind one bit. I decided to forgo kissing her, knowing the real romance would come later. I was learning not to rush things the way I had with other women.

We said our goodnights, and she left the car a happy woman. I took off, bathed in something I could not describe. But the smile on my face said it all.

Alone in my bedroom, I contacted my demon spirits and asked them why Rachael was so special, so different from the other women I had dated.

An answer came fast: She's just a nice girl. You have nothing to worry about.

Nothing to worry about, they said. But a message in the back of my mind kept playing over and over. It was the warning to be careful about her ex-boyfriend. That was when I began planning my battle strategy.

Rachael and I had many memorable dates together, inseparable times, even nights when I just parked in front of her home for hours—we didn't know how to say goodbye to each other.

A Mysterious Night

One night Rachael called and asked what I was doing. What I was doing was resting from the previous night of wild partying with another woman I'd been dating. As soon as I told her I was staying home, she invited herself over. She lived in my neighborhood, so I knew there would be a knock on my door soon.

Five minutes later, I opened the door and there was Rachael and a little girl, her two-year-old daughter, Sarah. I led my two guests to the living room where they made themselves comfortable on the couch.

After flicking on the TV, I went to the kitchen to fetch some sodas and munchies, returning with a small plastic bowl for Sarah to eat out of so she wouldn't drop crumbs onto her nice clothes.

Sarah started eating the munchies but turned away from me to her mother.

"Mommy, let's go home."

"Now?" said her mother.

Rachael didn't understand what was wrong, but I knew. The young child had picked up the bad vibes from the unclean spirits in the apartment.

Rachael spotted some of my religious paraphernalia lying around that spoke of *espiritismo*, Santeria, and Palo and asked what I was into. I told her she had nothing to worry about. All I did was burn candles. Thirty minutes later, I walked her home. That was when she revealed to me that her parents, Robert and Anna, were born-again Christians and that she at one time had gone to church with them. Now she was a back-slider, seeking that which she had left, she said: the love and power of Jesus Christ.

"How deep are you involved?" she asked, her dark eyes filled with concern.

"In what?"

"Witchcraft."

She had me. I turned to her with a reassuring smile. "Look, you don't have to worry. All I'm doing is burning candles to Catholic saints. No harm in that, right?"

That was when the backslider started to preach to me. "The Bible says you shouldn't worship anything or anyone except Jesus Christ. What you're doing is called idolatry."

I let out a loud, defensive laugh. "You're so old-fashioned and funny. If you want to know the truth, the Bible was put together by forty losers who had nothing better to do than to create a money-laundering religion."

Rachael looked at me strangely and without a word walked away. It would be days before we saw each other again or even talked on the phone. I decided to break the long silence with one call. The line rang and rang, and finally someone picked it up. It was her. A sincere hello from me was all it took to start a string of restaurant dinners and movie matinees over the course of several weekends. We were spending more time together than ever.

Back into My Own World

After weeks of dating, I dropped out of sight again, and some time went by when I didn't see Rachael at all. The reason was because the other women in my life kept me busy. I was in and out of bars and caught up with the things of the religion: attending demonic parties, doing spiritual ceremonies, and casting spells on anyone I wanted. One day out of the blue Rachael called just to chat.

"What are you doing this evening?" she asked.

"Staying home to take care of personal matters."

Again she invited herself over, and I couldn't tell her no. I liked her so much, yet didn't know why. "Come over around nine o'clock," I told her. By then I would be finished with what I was doing.

When Rachael arrived, I grabbed the phone and ordered takeout. I fed a rented movie into my VCR as soon as she set up our food so we could eat. During the flick, I saw in her eyes that she had something important to say.

"John, I know that both of us have been dating others. However, you are always on my mind, and I know that you feel the same way."

What could I say? I couldn't fool her anymore. I didn't want to. What I wanted was her. But I loved the dark side, the power it brought, and the beautiful women it attracted. She had made a stabbing confession, and her declaration for us to solely focus on each other was a bold move. I respected her for that, so I told her yes. But could I really do it? Could I commit myself to a woman whose parents were "born-again" Christians without a high priest from the religion taking me out in one swift act of vengeance? I told her there were going to be a lot of disappointed women wishing they could have me back.

After the movie, I walked Rachael home. Her boldness had impressed me so much that along the way I decided to do some gut-spilling myself.

"Rachael, I need to tell you the truth about myself." I had her attention. "I'm a *Santero* and a *Palero Tata*—a devil worshipper." I went on to tell her about the supernatural ceremonies, the animal sacrifices, the witchcraft parties, and the powers I possessed. "If people could see the evil that's veiled from their eyes, what tarot reading does to a person, and the danger parents put upon their children by getting them involved in Halloween, they would shriek in horror." I also added that the only way for me to get out of what I was doing was to have a death curse placed upon me.

"John, I don't care how deeply you are involved in this witchcraft. I love you and want us to be together."

Rachael and I continued going out, weekend after weekend, doing what everyone else did. But when we weren't together, I went to my witchcraft parties and other dark events, sacrificing animals to the demon gods in ceremony rituals for new recruits. I was proud of what I did. Satan was my father. I loved smelling liquor, cigars, and rotten animal blood. It was my life and my destiny.

History Repeats Itself

With my ex-wife Mari moving up the ranks in Santeria, Amanda followed, and in a ceremony involving the reading of shells—*caracoles*—a bid was placed over her head in the religion. Now history was repeating itself.

My daughter was being dedicated to the gods just as I was when I was ten years old. What had been done to me as a little boy was now being done to her. I wasn't given a choice or an opportunity to think it over, and the same thing was happening to her. How often things repeat themselves in life. Snatched out of the hands of my mother, now Amanda was being snatched out of my hands to be given over to Santeria and *espiritismo*. Shortly afterward, Amanda was crowned the sole possession of *Ochun* and *Obatala*: a pair of evil spirits. From here on the spirits of *espiritismo* and Santeria would have control of her life, offering her a purpose and a destiny.

As the days and weeks went by, I prepared myself for a gathering with the spirits that took place every six months to see where I stood in the religion. I was summoned to stand before a clan of spirits. That night as I stood in the basement for my ritual, I could feel the presence of every demon entering the room for the ceremony. As the ritual began, it was like a parent looking over a child's report card. If everything went well, it meant the powers vested in me were still flowing and any outsider who threatened me would easily be brought down. I preferred the term "taken out." It commanded respect. If I didn't stand well in the reading, a restoration cleansing was in order, followed by a demonic feast. But if I were a complete reprobate to the religion, I could be punished with either a broken arm or leg, depending on how obstinate I was. Or a demon would punish me and I would end up in the hospital with a long-term illness. And if a greater punishment was warranted, something else would happen, leading to death.

That night I sat in the center of the basement. Behind my chair was placed a glass of water with a flower in it and a white candle. As the reading took place, every demon showed up to give a report of my spiritual contract with them, my responsibility to the contract, and what other levels I needed to reach.

The medium performing the ritual said, "*Siete Rayos* is here, and he said he's happy with you. *Zarabanda* is here, and he said he is happy to have you as a son. *Candelo*, the spirit father of Haiti is also here, and he said how much he loves you. *El Indio* also just came in, and he said how proud he is of you and the rank that you hold in *espiritismo*. They're asking me right now if you have any questions for them."

"I don't have any questions," I said with a big smile on my face.

As for my "report card" that night, I got an A. Aunt Maria was so proud of me. She had been serving the religion for fifty years. But a good report didn't mean I was safe. I had enemies in the religion who would always try to take me out no matter how good I stood with the demonic spirits. The reason? Jealousy, due to the powers I possessed.

Betwixt Two Worlds

Something began happening to me that no one knew about. I was depressed, angry, and bitter, and the emptiness that churned within me like a storm-ravaged sea was driving me crazy. Where had I deviated? I was still sacrificing animals to my demon gods and still casting spells. The answer to the problem came to me when I was called to attend a witchcraft ceremony one night. Mari and I had discussed a few days earlier that I would pick up

Amanda that night and spend time with her because she had been asking for me.

As I was on my way out the door, the phone rang. It was Aunt Maria. "John, what are you doing?"

"I'm on my way to pick up Amanda," I told her.

"Stop what you're doing and come straight to the house. We have an emergency *mesa blanca* meeting, and it needs to be done tonight. I was told by the spirits that you must be here at this meeting."

"But, Aunt Maria, I promised Amanda I would spend time with her. I don't want to break my promise."

"Well, you can see her later, or maybe you can see her sometime tomorrow, but you need to get here now."

So that night I went straight to the meeting of the *mesa blanca*.

My heart was sorrowful because I was betwixt two worlds, the world of being a father to my daughter and the commitment that drove me, contract after contract, to be part of a world that many only dreamed of. I was too busy to visit the only person in the world who resembled me and whom I truly loved. Many times I felt like I was incarcerated behind invisible prison bars like the people I had entrapped into the religion.

Chapter 11

The Son of the Devil Exposed

Rachael and I continued seeing each other, but the nightclubs and drinking had stopped—at least for her. I was allowed to visit Rachael, but on her parents' terms. We had dinners at their home and watched movies with her younger brother. That's all we did.

Robert and Anna were, and still are, hardcore, hallelujah Christians. Each time I called on Rachael, I was subjected to their ranting sermons on the Bible and Jesus. So in order to keep them happy, I said yes to them, nodding at everything they told me with secret disdain. But this is what helped cover up who I was. Rachael had not yet told her parents about my devilish ways. They only knew me, John Ramirez, the young man interested in their daughter. I could see the truth would come out one day, and when it did, I wondered how they would receive me then.

Plenty of family dinners and home-dates with Rachael eventually did something good—it brought us all closer. Gone was the unfamiliar face I wore each time I visited and the uneasiness of waiting for someone to say something first at the dinner table.

Even though we were all more comfortable with each other, every time they talked to me about this Jesus person, my blood went cold and I cringed. I felt like jumping across the table and choking them to death. If they only knew that the world I lived in was a lot stronger than theirs.

One night at the dinner table, Anna looked at me and said, "John, do you know how much Jesus loves you?"

I looked over at her and grinned. "Yeah, yeah, I heard that before."

"Well, I just want to share with you the love of Jesus."

"You already told me, so I think I already know."

She smiled. "You know that Jesus died for you, right John."

"This Jesus thing you're talking to me about, He's nothing but a bully. I don't know what kind of God He is, or what kind of love you're talking about."

"Why would you say something like that, John?" Anna asked.

"You think you're the only one that really knows the Bible. What about what He did to that man called Job? What kind of God is that, giving the devil permission to destroy his family, giving the devil permission to destroy his home? You call that love? If you call that love, I don't need that kind of love, so keep it to yourself. That's not love at all. That's just pure evil."

"But, John, He was just testing Job."

"That's not a test," I said, disgusted. "That's just being brutal. So keep this Jesus to yourself."

With the summer and fall months leading to winter, my relationship with Rachael deepened, and

Anna and Robert got to like me even more, despite our differences regarding God. But that was because they didn't know who I was. What I stood for. The talk of an upcoming banquet sponsored by the church they attended got everyone excited. Everyone but me, because now I understood where Rachael's strength lay. It came from her praying parents. That was the reason my powers couldn't affect her, and why I had failed to convert her to the religion.

As soon as I got invited to the banquet, I felt a warning shot go through me like a bolt of lightning. So I decided to go summon the demons through my god-mother Aunt Maria to ask permission to attend this church banquet.

"Go, there's nothing to worry about. You are well protected by *espiritismo*, Santeria, and Palo," she said. "No one can do anything to you because you are more powerful than they are." My aunt's response relaxed me so much that now I felt better about going. In fact, I was looking forward to it.

Hanging with the Hallelujah People

Arriving at the hall on the night of the banquet, we pushed past thick, glass doors as Robert and Anna led the way through a carpeted foyer with elegant chandeliers overhead. I followed with Rachael, her arm threaded through mine. At a check-in place, a hostess took our coats and on we went, weaving our way through crowds of people, hundreds of them, until we entered a spacious dining area where dozens of banquet tables were covered in fine cloth, as white as the glittering lights overhead.

Standing in a sea of churchgoers, I was introduced to people on my right and people on my left, all sincere-looking folks.

Rachael turned to a couple and said, "Mike and Maria, this is my boyfriend John."

They smiled. "Nice to meet you, John. Welcome to the banquet."

I gave them a mysterious smile and just said, "Thank you."

No one seemed to notice how I was dressed, and if they did they didn't show it. I had come in solid dark clothes—black as a crow—so that the power of demons could protect me from anything that was there.

Once inside the grand ballroom, we were led to our assigned table. Around us, people who had not seen each other in awhile hugged, kissed, and smiled. It was the craziest thing I ever saw. What a bunch of nuts! I couldn't understand why people were God-blessing each other. No one was sneezing.

Near our table, Rachael turned to a young lady. "Hi, Marisa, this is John."

When I went to shake hands with her, the girl said, "I know you from somewhere. I've seen you before. I know I know you."

"Well, I don't know you," I said, trying to be polite.

She was stunned and amazed, and she kept repeating, "No, I know you...I know you," as I walked away and took my seat.

At the head of the ballroom, a live band played. They were all skilled musicians with great voices, but their lyrics had to do with holy living, loving thy neighbor, and the Bible—things that made me uncomfortable.

One of the men on the platform, a tall, nice-looking guy wearing a cream-colored suit, appeared to be the leader of the group. And when he lifted his voice to the instruments playing behind him, some people rose from their seats, marched to the front, and danced like fools. It was so stupid I wanted to laugh. *They must be drunk*, I thought. But there was no liquor anywhere in sight.

With every guitar strum, tambourine rattle, and hum of the synthesizer, something began happening to me. I was being subdued by something greater than all the demons I had ever known. How could this be? I was one of the highest-ranked warlocks in voodoo, possessed by unspeakable powers. Nothing could shake me. But there I was, little by little, moment by moment, being drawn to the music's message. Responding to wholesome, rhythmic beats.

When the singing paused for a break, dozens of large, aluminum containers were placed over flaming canisters on a train of tables against the wall opposite the stage. I had never seen so much food in all my life. This was truly a banquet. Tables were called out by number, and soon I was in a long line of people with Rachael ahead of me and Anna and Robert behind me. That was when I panicked.

Standing before us in line was a woman I hadn't seen in a long time. She was from the same occult inner-circle I was in. Only now, she was no longer part of the occult. Where had she been, and why hadn't I seen her anymore at the cult meetings? She had been missing for five years. She was one of my enemies for having left the religion. As soon as this woman turned my way, I hid behind Rachael. But my six-foot-two frame was difficult to conceal no matter what crowd I was in.

She greeted me. "Hello, John. How are you?"

I greeted her back. "I'm fine." I sensed the confrontation between good and evil on the line.

I turned to Rachael and whispered, "This woman knows I'm a devil worshipper because she came out of the same religious inner-circle that I'm involved in. I'm afraid she's going to blow my cover by telling your parents."

"Don't worry," Rachael said. "She won't say anything. I know her, and she's a good woman."

We got our food and walked back to our table. With everyone eating, I relaxed some. I had just dodged a bullet. But for how long would I be able to play hide-and-seek and get away with it? How long would my luck last? It didn't last very long, because unknown to me, in the distance of the ballroom, another set of eyes fell upon me. This time it was a man, someone else who had departed from the religion five years ago as well.

This person dragged Rachael's dad straight to the men's room.

"Do you have any idea who your daughter is dating?"

"Yeah, that's John," Robert said. "He's a nice guy."

"No, he's not!" the man said. "He is one of the biggest devil worshippers in New York City. He's into *espiritismo*, Santeria, and Palo. The reason I know that is because my Lord and Savior Jesus Christ set me free from that occult, which they call the religion. John was my buddy at one time, but not anymore. Now he's crazy and dangerous. Everyone knows about him. I'm surprised you don't. If I were you, I'd keep Rachael away from him."

Robert was shocked and didn't know what to say, but he came back to the table as if nothing had happened.

The day after the banquet, Rachael and her parents got into it at their home. "Your relationship with John ends now!" her mother demanded.

"But why?" Rachael asked.

"Because he's involved in witchcraft."

"John isn't going to hurt me."

"What if he hurts Sarah?" Robert said.

"He loves Sarah."

"How can you be sure?" Anna asked with anguish. "Everyone who knows him says he's crazy."

And it was true. No one from my neighborhood wanted problems with me. They had heard what *Santeros* could do when crossed. Casting spells was only the beginning.

Rachael stormed out of the house, ignoring her parents' warning, went to a pay phone, and called me frantically. "My parents know all about you and asked me not to see you anymore! But I refused to stop seeing you."

"Rachael, everything will be okay," I said, trying to soothe her.

We continued to date. I took her to restaurants, art shows, and plays. But not to bars or nightclubs. I had stopped doing that with her. But what I didn't stop doing was practicing the religious duties in *espiritismo*, because if I did the same demons I worshipped would turn against me.

The Devil Has No Respect

Rachael's strained relationship with her parents began to affect us. And the more she reminded me, the more I started to despise her.

"What you're doing is evil in the eyes of God," she said.

"What do you know? You're a backslider."

"Stop it, John. I can't keep seeing someone my parents disapprove of."

"So, we'll stop seeing each other. It'll give me more time to do what I want."

"Your religion," she said. "That's all you care about."

"That's right. I've got to please my demons. I met them before meeting you. The only person who's taking up space in my life is you."

Rachael turned away in anger. But she would never get rid of me. She needed me to protect her from the lunatic idiot she called her ex-lover, even though at the moment I was not in good standing with Robert and Anna.

One evening, Rachael and I went to her parents' house to pick up Sarah and bring her home. Sarah was acting strange in Anna and Robert's house, and I knew right away something was wrong with her spiritually. As we headed to Rachael's apartment, walking down the street, the street was cold and lonely.

As every streetlamp illuminated the street, I kept looking at Sarah in the stroller, knowing that it wasn't her anymore. The child kept staring at me with a very demonic look, so much that Rachael caught on. She knew Sarah was no longer in the carriage. Something evil had taken over, and she was only three years old.

When we got to Rachael's place, I tried entertaining Sarah, stalling for time to see what was going to happen. I got on my hands and knees to give her a pony ride, but Sarah stood at a distance, staring at me with a sharp, evil look. I knew this was a demonic attack. A witchcraft spell, sent to harm Rachael or myself. But because I was powerful, it couldn't do anything to me. Sad to say, because Sarah was the weakest link, it took over her little body, including her mind and thoughts. Now I had a fight on my hands. Rachael was very alarmed but quiet. What had gotten in her daughter was an old, demonic spirit. And all this was happening because Sarah's dad, Mr. Ex, was trying to put a spell on my relationship with Rachael. I finally left Rachael's place and headed home, but afterwards all hell broke loose.

Rachael called me first thing the next day, her voice trembling.

"John, John, you don't know what happened to Sarah and me last night after you left."

"Tell me, what happened?" I said.

"As soon as you were gone, I sensed a heavy presence hovering over my apartment. I grabbed Sarah and we went into the bathroom to take a shower to shake things off. But things got worse. As we were coming out of the bathroom, I looked into my living room. The same fear gripped me again, but this time even worse. My blood went cold and I tried to scream, but nothing came out of my mouth—something had me by the throat. I saw this monster, like a four-legged animal with fiery red eyes, sitting in my living room. I knew that was the devil himself, sitting there waiting for my daughter and me. As I grabbed Sarah to run into my bedroom and close the door behind me, I felt that thing get up and try to chase us into the room. I slammed the door and started to call on the name of Jesus. Once I did that, it was gone. What is going on, John?"

"This all has to do with your ex," I said. "I had nothing to do with it. But I'll tell you what, just because it affected Sarah, he will pay the price. I will make sure he gets punished beyond what he could ever imagine."

I hung up the phone.

Chapter 12

The Setup

One night I received an unexpected phone call from Robert.

"Hey, John, my wife and I are having a prayer service in our house on Saturday afternoon about one o'clock, and we would like you to come. Please be here."

"Well, what kind of meeting are you talking about?" I asked.

"Just some church members getting together to pray."

"Okay, I'll be there." I knew this was my chance to confront Ray, the man who spilled the beans about me at the banquet. It was my opportunity to get revenge. This meeting would give me a chance to mock and challenge those who claimed they were Christian. I would cling to my *espiritismo* and evil powers during the time I was at the gathering. How entertaining that would be. I would be in control of it all, and no one would ever know.

That Saturday afternoon, one by one they came: smiles on their faces, God's praises on their lips. Men shook hands and clapped each other's shoulders while women hugged and kissed one another on the cheek. These people really loved each other. Later I would discover the reason was because they lived by a different Spirit, for a different cause, under another name, a man named Jesus. They said He walked on water, healed the sick, spoke truth, and died on Good Friday. No one from the religion believed anything like this. The principles of *espiritismo* just didn't teach such things.

When everyone settled down, the group of Christians, about fifteen people in all, stood to their feet in a circle, held hands, and began to pray, one person at a time. It was so orderly. I thought it strange they didn't pray for themselves but for each other. Even people who weren't there were prayed for—brothers and sisters from their faith who were physically ill, and others in need of God's intervention. This was crazy. What kind of people went around calling themselves brothers and sisters? Shedding tears for one another?

After a round of applause and cries of hallelujahs, the person next to me shouted about how Jesus changed his life, and everyone sat down to hear his testimony. "I'll never be the same," the man said.

I would have challenged him right then and there, but a demon began revealing things to me, personal things about everyone there. Right then, one of the older men—a man they called an "elder"—started to say things to the people. As he went around the room, he told church members about the goodness, love, and plan that Jesus had for their lives. As he drew near to me, I was already half demon-possessed. He pointed a finger at me and told me Jesus loved me and died for me on the cross to give me a new life. Then he said, "Jesus is calling you. What are you waiting for?"

At that moment, I wanted to leap from my seat and choke the life out of him. My blood went ice cold, and I could feel the fire within me. What nerve he had to speak to me that way. If he only knew I had the power the take him out at any given time, he would never have pointed a finger at me. He was beneath me. The old man's eyes locked into me as if someone had given him authority. He wasn't the quiet old man anymore. The spiritual battle between me and the elder came to a halt when he motioned to the pastor to pray.

I couldn't wait for the meeting to be over because my eyes were on that blabber-mouth, the one who had told Robert and Anna about my life in the religion.

When the gathering ended with a prayer and a few hallelujahs, people started to embrace each other while I was getting ready to attack. As soon as my eyes pierced across the room, I targeted Ray and made my way over. My first words were, "How are you doing, Ray?"

He fidgeted and replied in a nervous voice, "I'm fine."

I looked him up and down. "The reason I came to this meeting was to see you. To discuss the comments you made about me at the banquet to Rachael's dad. Did you think for a second I wasn't going to find out?"

"I was nervous and didn't know what to do," he said. "The evening I saw you, fear gripped me and I thought—oh my God, these witches are having their own banquet next door to ours. That's when I panicked and told someone. And who better than Robert? But I'm so sorry for what happened."

We shook hands. "Don't you ever let something like this happen again."

I departed to the kitchen where they were serving brunch.

Later, Rachael and I met up and she asked me, "What did you think of the prayer meeting?"

"It was…okay." I really didn't want to discuss it. I was accustomed to casting spells, winning battles, and watching gullible people succumb to whatever curses I placed on them. But today, for the first time, I had experienced something different, and all regarding a Spirit that was not only powerful, but gentle as well. They called the Spirit the Holy Ghost. But I was still filled with questions. Things I didn't want to share with anyone.

A few days later I found myself confronting a Jehovah's Witness in the neighborhood running her mouth off about how this Jesus died on a tree. How dare she spill such erroneous information! She got her story dead wrong.

"Listen to me, lady," I said. "What do you know about this Jesus man? You know nothing. He died on a cross."

"But the cross was a tree," she said.

I turned around and said, "No, it was a cross. How foolish are you, lady?" My blood started to boil and my temperature began to rise. I wanted to grab her by the throat and shake some sense into her. I couldn't believe myself as I snapped out of it. *What am I doing? I'm a devil worshipper. How can I be defending this guy named Jesus?*

"Get your story straight next time," I spat out as I turned away from the lady and walked down the sidewalk. As I left I was embarrassed with myself, defending someone I did not serve or believe in. How crazy I was!

The Visitation

It happened one lazy afternoon while I was home watching TV. My back was reclined, and my legs kicked up, when a voice that wasn't part of the dialogue on the screen spoke. This voice seemed to emanate from somewhere beyond the living room, yet it sounded so near.

I jumped from the couch and wheeled around at the four walls but saw no one. Yet somehow I knew I was being watched. Then the voice spoke again. And this time every hair on my body stood at attention: *My son, I am coming soon. What are you planning to do with yourself?*

The voice wasn't from any demon. This voice was different from any voice I had ever known. The best way I could describe it was the awesome peace I experienced that was beyond human comprehension. Like standing at a brook and hearing its current passing by.

Seconds later, my eyes were led across my living room to a vision of a blazing sky, like a ball of fire, while people on earth screamed and ran in fear for their lives. I tried to make sense of it all, but at the same time I wanted to shake it off like it never happened. I waited with petrified amazement until the strange vision disappeared. Seeing something that amazing left a need in my heart.

A few days later I couldn't hold it in anymore, and I confronted Robert about what happened in my living room. As I explained to him, he said, "Jesus is calling you, John. Jesus loves you."

"You're crazy, you know that?" I said, laughing it off. "I finally came to the conclusion that you're crazy. No one is calling me."

His message to me was clear. The choice to surrender to God was mine. No one could make it for me. I could either continue yielding to the devil, worshipping him and his demons, or I could give my life to Jesus and let Him have full control. But was I willing to part with the position I held in *espiritismo* under threat of death? Was I ready to stop doing what I loved? Did I really want God to change me? I was so confused that when I went home that night, I didn't consult the resident demons in my bedroom. Instead, the next night I arranged a meeting with Aunt Maria.

As we sat at her kitchen table, she said, "John, what seems to be the problem?"

"I'm tired of these hallelujah people saying that we're evil and they're the good ones," I said.

My aunt stayed silent, her eyes focused on me.

"Aunt Maria, did you hear what I said? Why are we the bad ones and they are the good ones? Could you answer my question?"

Aunt Maria turned her eyes away from me. "I've been a devil worshipper since I was a little girl, and I'm glad that I have these powers and I can defend myself and hurt those who want to hurt me."

I knew in my heart that Aunt Maria couldn't answer the question, and I realized that maybe these church people knew something I didn't know. For the first time, I felt ashamed and dirty being part of this thing called the religion. I walked away feeling sorrowful, empty, and confused.

Stepping into the Light

Time went by and once again Rachael's parents extended an invitation they had prayed I would accept: to visit their church.

I laughed. "You're kidding, right?"

But they asked me to think it over. So I told them I would. Since when did I care about other people's feelings? I was only interested in me, how to descend deeper into the abyss of hell, how to do greater things than anyone in the religion had ever done. Yet little by little, moment by moment, my resistance was breaking down. Lately I had found myself unable to say no to such simple invitations. First it was the banquet, then the prayer meeting, and now church. When would I stop giving in? When would this strange urge quit drawing me to places I hated to be in?

Several Sundays passed without Rachael's parents getting a commitment from me. Then one day I decided to accept their invitation. For the first time in my life I stepped into an evangelical church service—without permission from the demon spirits that controlled my life. For the first time in twenty-five years, I was on my own.

Chapter 13

Mr. Rogers' Neighborhood

Walking through the doors of Grace and Mercy Fellowship that Sunday morning, I thought I had stepped into Mr. Rogers' Neighborhood. Everyone behaved so squeaky clean that it bugged the heck out of me. How could a bunch of people with different color skin and from different social and economic backgrounds all get along? Only in a make-believe world could something like this occur. Mr. Rogers' Neighborhood was an appropriate name for where I was, and I wasn't going to change it. I walked in with a smirk on my face, ready for any challenge.

"John, I've got a surprise for you," Rachael said.

"Really? What is it?"

She dug into her handbag and pulled out a large black book.

I thought I was dreaming, but no, there it was in my hands: a black, leather-bound King James Version of the Holy Bible with gold-trimmed edges on every page. All sixty-six books. I didn't want to hurt her feelings, so I accepted it. I said to myself, *She must be crazy thinking I'm going to keep this and read it. I haven't seen a Bible in twenty-five years. This is for people who are weak to carry around.*

As the weeks went by Rachael's parents kept pressuring me with invitations to attend another church service with them. A miracle would have to happen for me to go with them again. But one Friday evening, it did.

Rachael and her parents begged me to go to another church service with them where people shared testimonies about how their lives were transformed. During that time, an usher came across the sanctuary toward me. He leaned over and asked, "Can I pray for you?"

Quick as lightning, a demon showed up to protect me. I looked at him and said, "Get out of my face with your prayer."

Rachael was shocked, and we started to argue right there in church.

"Why didn't you let him pray for you?" she said.

"I didn't feel like it. Let him go pray for someone else. I don't need any prayer."

She rolled her eyes at me, and for the rest of the evening we didn't speak to each other.

But on Sunday morning, I got up early and prepared myself to attend church with Rachael and Sarah.

After psyching myself to believe I was going to a party, I threw my Bible in a brown paper bag so that people in the neighborhood wouldn't see me carrying it. What would they say if they caught me with the thing? The whole community was aware of me being a devil worshipper. How foolish it would look for a true devil worshipper who had everyone in the neighborhood living in fear to carry a Bible? What a contradiction.

Services started at 10 a.m. I guided my car to the curb, extracted my Bible from the paper bag, and stepped into the church building.

First stop: Bible class. And the place was full. What had I gotten myself into?

After Bible class came the worship service. It was there I began feeling unusually sick. That's when I realized my demon powers had kicked in, even with people all around singing praises to God. I knew the demons were trying to get my attention.

A person next to me turned to me and whispered, "Hey, are you okay? You don't look well. You look kind of pale."

"No, I'm okay…I'm fine."

I tried to shake the feeling off, turning my attention back to the preacher on the platform.

Some Sundays when services ran long, I didn't understand what was going on or what was being said. There were some simple truths about Bible doctrine I couldn't grasp. But for the most part, being in church felt therapeutic. I was experiencing something I had never found in *espiritismo*—a genuine love demonstrated to me from members of the congregation.

The Man in the Mirror

The more I attended church, the more I began to like Bible class. It was something new to me. Different from the routine of devil worshipping and killing animals. But as much as I liked church, I loved the dark side more. And the main reason was because it gave me something I didn't have as a boy: the image of a real father. One who was supposed to hug me, kiss me, and tell me how proud he was of me. Someone who should have asked, "How are things in school?" A role model to help me believe in myself and push me to become a man of virtue. A dad in whom I could take pause and reflect on the good memories he should have left for me and my brothers: trips to the park, a swim in the pool, bicycle rides. A man I could feel a sense of protection from, one who was supposed to make my mother smile instead of making her suffer. But no matter, I had a substitute—a relationship with Lucifer, the devil. He was my real father. And whenever I needed advice and guidance, I would go to him for answers.

Sometimes I wondered what I was doing by going to church. I would sit in the corner of the sanctuary and think to myself, *What am I looking for? Everything I own I have obtained through witchcraft, and the more involved I become, the more I get. If I need another job, or money to buy clothes for my daughter, all I have to do is worship the devil and it is mine. I have it made.* But I wasn't happy because the relationships I'd once had now were falling apart. One of the dearest persons in my life was my mother. I knew she loved me unconditionally, and that I would forever be her son. But I was too far gone down the path of devils and demons for her to reach out to me and take me back into her arms the way she used to when I was a boy. I was a man now and had no time to receive motherly affection, or even the friendship of my own brothers. I was only able to relate to those who lived crazy like me, bowing down to *espiritismo*, Santeria, and Palo. In that world, my distrust for people caused me to reject family and friends until they became as strangers. Who would be the next person I would estrange myself from?

Sometimes the emptiness I felt inside hurt so bad laughter fled from me, and all I wanted to do was cry. Where were the demons I had worshipped for so long? Oh, they were still around. But this time, instead of infusing me with the power to overcome my problems, my problems were overcoming me. I was no longer a husband, and I was an absent dad. Suddenly all the witchcraft parties I'd attended, all the spells I had cast on unsuspecting people and sneaking into mental hospitals, all the years it took for me to attain the high rank I held in the religion now made me realize what a prideful, hateful, malicious, slanderous person I had become, especially to those who called themselves Christians. How I wanted to destroy them. Satan had offered his power to me on a fishhook, and I took it, thinking I could have the greatest thing anyone could possess, when in reality I possessed nothing. Satan possessed me. And he had no intentions of letting go. What I thought was his hand of protection on me was really a viselike grip I could not escape. How I wanted to find the key to the invisible shackles on my wrists and ankles. How I longed to be free.

With all this goodness and kindness flowing my way, I still found myself within the inner circle of fellow cult members during the course of the week. It was what I craved. Those at the religion didn't mind one bit that I attended a place of worship different from theirs. In fact, they weren't even offended. They knew I wouldn't betray them or any of the demons from the religion. They knew where my loyalty stood—with them. But with all that, I was still being drawn to church from time to time. Still caught between two worlds—light and darkness.

The Truth Calling

Many nights, alone in my apartment with my daughter, I still wrestled with the strange heaviness that created a sorrow in me and made my eyes pool with tears, all the while fighting back the on-rush of emotions because I didn't want Amanda to see her old man cry. What kind of a man was I? And what had I really done with my life that would make my daughter Amanda proud of me one day? All I was good for was witchcraft, guzzling booze, and chasing women.

If Amanda was the one with tears in her eyes, I would've rushed to her, put my arms around her, and comforted her. But who did I have at that moment that would comfort me? That's when I felt a prompting to call an older woman from the church who was like a grand-mother to all. So I did. I was so grateful she lived just a few blocks away. I waited until she picked up the phone. I was so desperate to talk to someone, anyone. But it had to be her because she was a godly, Christian woman.

Finally, her voice broke through like a ray of sun-light. She was so glad to hear it was me.

"Please lead me to the Lord," I begged. "I want to pray to take the pain away."

"I would love to, John," she answered.

She invited me over to her place, and I was out of the house as soon as I hung up the phone, taking Amanda with me. I was heading in the wrong direction down the street and didn't want to admit it—lost just like my soul and about to split hell wide open. I had been to the woman's house once before. Why couldn't I find it now?

It was dark and late, and as I hustled past lamp-lit streets with Amanda by the hand, I looked for a pay phone.

"Daddy, are you okay? Why are we rushing?" she said.

"Everything's going to be fine, Amanda." My eyes darted around for a phone booth. "Do you trust me? I trust you."

"Yes, Daddy."

"Do you love me? I love you."

"Yes, Daddy, I love you."

"Okay, everything's going to be all right."

Happily, I found a pay phone, fed a quarter into the slot, and dialed the number. My hands were shaking, my breathing ragged. My patience strained, waiting for a ring. They say a man never asks for directions. But I was desperate. At the sound of a clunk I realized I had lost twenty-five cents and the call, so I ran to another booth and pumped in another quarter. The same thing happened. I slammed the receiver into the cradle, the urge to cry rising within. Someone was making it hard for me to find the address—to have the truth. That's when I started thinking about going back home. But the voice that had spoken to that time in my living room wouldn't let me. *"Don't give up,"* it said. So I moved on with a determined pace.

At last I found the building. In no time I was in the old woman's living room, sitting on her sofa, Amanda at my side. I wanted prayer for her too.

The woman said, "John, we can stand and hold hands, and I will pray for you and Amanda. Jesus wants to be the Lord of your life. Is that what you want?"

"Yes, that's what I want," I said. The surge of tears got stronger, rising like a mighty tide.

A few members of her family surrounded me and began to pray. I felt at peace, but in the back of my mind I was very much aware that my demon tormentors were not far away, hunting me down. Lost in the intercession, I saw myself again as a nine-year-old boy. I had gotten off the bus at Fordham Road and was on my way home when I ran into an evangelical street meeting. There people were witnessing and giving out tracts. Some kind soul asked if I wanted prayer and I said yes. What joy I had in my heart. But because I didn't have anyone to direct my life or take me to church, something else did the directing for me. A better word was *misdirected*.

As the people prayed for me, I said the prayers from my lips but not from my heart. I couldn't come to the full submission, accepting Jesus as my Savior, knowing the contract of twenty-five years of my life that was signed over to the devil and his demons. I went back home that night with my daughter, trying to make sense of everything that had taken place, with many unanswered questions.

The next time I saw the old woman in church, she counseled me about totally renouncing witchcraft and getting rid of all the paraphernalia in my apartment. If she only knew that in my heart I didn't fully surrender to God because I was scared of being labeled a traitorous enemy by the religious members of *espiritismo*, Santeria, and Palo, and would no doubt have a death contract put out on me as soon as they discovered what was in my heart.

Now, in order to honor the commitment I made long ago with the dark side, I guarded the biggest secret I had ever kept—that I was falling in love with Jesus. But I could not fool those who knew my personal history since I was ten years old. It didn't matter that I carried a Bible or went to church. To them, I was still the devil man. And how right they were. Even though I was prayed for by Christians, I kept attending the witchcraft world.

Chapter 14

Demon-Possessed in Church

One Sunday I decided to go back to Grace and Mercy Church on 170th Street and Jerome Avenue. I went back because in my heart I knew on the night I went to the old lady's house and prayed with her, my yes was not to commit myself to the Lord, but for Him to protect me from the demons I knew would hound me like bounty hunters. I walked past the spacious lobby and into the gymnasium where the services were held.

There must have been about two hundred people attending church that day. As the service began, I heard a voice speak into my ear. *What are you doing here?* I turned to see who it was. But all I saw were those who stood around me, people clapping their hands and stomping their feet to the rhythm of guitars and harmonic voices being lifted up to God in worship.

I dismissed it and fell in line with what the others were doing. But the enjoyment didn't last for long. Several minutes later, that same voice spoke stronger. *WHAT ARE YOU DOING HERE?* it repeated. A chill swept through my bones as if ice water flowed in my veins. They were coming for me. Hordes of them in the house of God.

Something came over me with an all-too-familiar feeling. It reached inside and took ground. This was followed by another and another, until I realized with horror that I was being raided by demon spirits, a house invasion of the worst kind—for the possession of my soul.

I started to feel physically sick and dropped to my seat hoping no one would notice the transformation taking place. I tried fighting back. But all I kept hearing was that voice: *You don't belong here. You belong to us!*

That's when the pastor took the microphone and stopped the worship. He addressed the congregation. "Beloved, I was just led by the Holy Spirit right now to make an emergency altar call for those that need it. So please come up to the front; the altar is open."

As I glanced around the sanctuary, I saw many people leave their seats and go up to the altar to be prayed for. I got the sudden urge to run to the altar, to flee from the things pursuing me. But I knew in my mind I was just going up there to shake off the demons, not to receive prayer at all. I walked to the front and stood alongside the others.

The pastor came down the line, praying for people one at a time. I was next to last in the long line of believers, hoping now that by the time it was my turn to be prayed for the demons would have fled and I could go happily back to my seat without incident. But the shorter the line got, and the closer the pastor approached, the more his face came into detail: brown eyes, thick mustache, graying temples. Now my legs strangely locked and I was unable to step away. I stood before the pastor shaking from the warring demons within. For the first time in twenty-five years I had no control over the inner hosts. They were controlling me.

The pastor leaned into me and whispered, "John, do you want prayer?"

I looked him in the eye and glared at him. "No, go to hell."

He gave me an astonished look, and I said, "I came here for you."

In that moment he knew it was no longer I who was confronting him, but the devil himself. An anger I had never known stirred from deep within like the rumblings of an active volcano, and before I knew it I was spewing profanity out of my mouth in a voice not my own. I was demon-possessed. *"Don't you dare touch him, mother---."*

Suddenly my hands felt like welded steel. I reached for the pastor's throat. It only took a moment for the vise-like grip coupled with the tremendous strength flowing through my body to lift him off the floor—legs kicking, eyes bulging, open mouth gasping for precious air. A pair of hands grabbed me from behind, trying to pull me away, and the war between good and evil broke out at the altar. Killing him would be a pleasure. I had never been this demon-possessed before and it thrilled me.

Twelve to fifteen men ran from their seats, trying to rescue the pastor. As I felt hands from all over tackling me, the men flew around like ragdolls, being tossed and thrown around the sanctuary.

To my dismay I felt the urge to run out of the building. I got as far as the door, looking to fly through the streets in the condition I was in. But something greater than me—greater than the demons—wouldn't allow it.

Back to the altar I returned for the kill. And as I did, a large group of men ran up behind me again and tried to grapple me to the floor.

"Joe, run this way!"

"Robert, Steve, come to the front now!"

"We need help!"

I felt myself reeling when someone climbed on my back. Then the weight of another person, and yet another, created a heap of bodies. I gained control of my balance, moving the huddle of men clamped around me from one side of the altar to the other with Herculean strength. Reversing my steps, I toppled someone to the floor, and a few more fell when I wrestled out of the grips that held my arms. Someone flew off my back like a rodeo rider on a wild stallion, and I flipped another person over when he grabbed at my neck. The power was exhilarating.

With the pastor in the clear, I lunged for him again. But this time something or someone came between us, a power greater than the one within me. Again I was tackled by the men, only to rise with ease, sweeping men three times my weight off me with effortless moves.

The mob of strong-armed men rolled back like weaklings, and someone else approached—Ray, the ex-witchcraft member from the very clan I was in. He didn't grab me or even try to touch me. He hugged me and said, "John, John, just say these words: Jesus is Lord! Just repeat these words, John. Jesus is Lord! Repeat them after me." I tried to speak but my lips had clamped shut as if someone had sewn them closed with needle and thread.

Tossing people off me, the struggle spun me toward an amazing sight: the congregation, a wall of people—saints of God—locked in loud intercessory prayer for me and warfare prayer against a host of demons. Every outstretched hand in the place caused me to weaken. The struggle at the altar ended when the words came out of my mouth: "Jesus is Lord."

Something flew out of me, and I felt deflated. The men still held me but not in a grappling hold like before. The force to subdue was over, and what remained were the voices of the men and women of the congregation—some weeping, some rejoicing, others speaking in a language I could not understand.

Drenched in sweat from the physical struggle, I was followed to the men's room by Ray, an usher named Tony, and another man. With my hair tousled and clothes disheveled, they wanted to make sure I was all right. I leaned against a sink, turned on the faucet, and threw water in my face, droplets falling from my brow to my nose to my chin. I waited for the questions I felt should have come my way from the three men standing beside me, but to my surprise they kept silent. What they wanted to know they would find out later.

Hell Returns to Church

The following Sunday I attended church as usual with some embarrassment and shame for what had happened the week before. All week long I had felt the demons' anger toward me. But I had had a taste of the goodness of Jesus, and for the first time the inescapable truth of the awful mess I was in came to me with a shuddering fear.

During Bible class, I was glad no one mentioned anything about the fiasco at the altar. And it was this that helped me to understand the love of Jesus in others. When the service started, I went and sat in my seat, taking in the presence of God while the worship team lifted up their voices in praise. What a good day to be alive.

When the music ended, we all sat and the associate pastor took the podium. But before he even said a word, I began to feel that same rage and sickness again. Something swirled behind me, around me, in me, and I ran to the altar for help.

As the pastor started his message, a pair of hands reached for his throat—my hands. Instantly, every able-bodied man in the congregation flew out of their seats in one mad rush to protect their pastor, to tear me away from him. It was the same scene happening all over again. In the huddle, the associate pastor tried praying for me, but I was too busy tossing grown men about.

Ushers flew off my back effortlessly. This was not what I had come to do, but they, the demons that had possessed me again, came for revenge a second time around. They were in full control of me. Hell came to church that day.

A fear I had never known raced through my mind as I realized Satan had no intentions of letting me go. He intended to make me his forever, whether I liked it or not, whether I served him or not. At that moment I cried out to Jesus. Not with my voice. My lips were stitched shut again. But within my heart—the place where only God hears.

A wall of men tried dragging me out of the sanctuary into the hallway, away from the altar, away from those who came to church that day, but burning hot energy surged through me, and more people tumbled away. A moment later, the intercessory prayers of the people began taking effect, and I was hustled out of the gym, subdued by the wave of men determined to see my deliverance. They called this type of prayer "spiritual warfare."

A legion of demonic spirits seeped out of me like air gushing from a balloon, and when everything was calm again, someone got a seat for me and I slumped into the chair. The pastor approached.

"John, how do you feel? Is everything okay now? Don't worry, everything's going to be all right."

What would I tell him? How could I explain that what I had just done was not really me? It was *them*, my so-called friends from the dark side coming to lay claim on me. I waited for an onslaught of questions, but instead what I got was a surge of the love of Jesus, a wall that would keep me from doing more damage that day. I was so humiliated, so ashamed of my uncontrollable actions. What label had I earned from these people? One thing was clear. If I didn't break the contract, I could count on the bounty-hunting demons visiting me again. The question was when.

To my surprise, I found myself back at church the following Sunday yet again, seeking answers to the awful ruckus I had created two weeks in a row. But something positive had happened in my life; otherwise I would have been attending a demonic service at the other church I belonged to that day.

At the end of another service, all the men of the church banded together and marched toward me. But it wasn't to tackle me to the floor. It was to present me with a gift. Tony, the man who had followed me to the bathroom after my first outburst, handed it to me and said, "The Lord has impressed upon our hearts to bless you with our congregational sweatshirt."

A warm feeling came over me. The men of the church considered me one of them. I choked back tears and the overwhelming feeling of acceptance that came with it. The blue sweatshirt was designed with the church's logo. It had my name embroidered on the front, and on the back a Roman helmet and gladiator's sword stood out beneath the arched word "Warriors." They told me it was a text from the Bible—Ephesians 6:17: "Take the helmet of salvation and the sword of the Spirit, which is the word of God." The message was clear. If I put on the helmet and wielded the sword the way I was supposed to, I would be able to withstand the attacks of the devil and his demons.

How could it be that people who didn't know me would show me this kind of love, knowing I was a devil-worshipper and not one of them?

Chapter 15

Jesus Takes Me to Hell

In the following weeks, a strong sense of bewilderment stirred within me. I was about to lose my mind. Who did I really belong to? As long as I continued to be pulled by the devil and wooed by the light, the tug-of-war would not let up. I knew I had to get rid of everything in my apartment that kept me tied to the religion and its demons.

As I paced around my apartment, going from room to room, I confronted the cauldron that was in the closet and the demonic symbols painted on the walls. I stared down into the cauldron, knowing what was in it—human bones and dried blood from the many animal sacrifices. My eyes darted across the room to the corner, where the statue of an Indian chief stood. We locked eyes, and for a moment it seemed as if his ceramic eyes came to life, burning with an unholy fire and hatred for me. A mounting tension welled within me from the many years I was faithful to the spirits. The smell of betrayal hung heavy in the air. But I was overcome by the strange power of the commitment I had made years ago. As long as I was in this state of mind, suspended between laughing and crying, the devil had me where he wanted—confused.

Nothing could clear my head now. Not the burning taste of liquor or advice from plastered friends at the bars; and nothing could fill my empty heart. Not the dim night-clubs that pounded with loud music or the sexy women who threw themselves at me. Nothing worked anymore. It was because I still felt a love and a commitment to the religion. I had lived in that world for twenty-five years. It was like a marriage, and now I sensed it was coming to an end. I was torn between two worlds. That night before going to bed, I felt spiritually drained. I had no strength in my body and no sense of direction. There was nothing left in me to the point that I thought about ending it all. As I went into my bedroom and switched off the lights, I sat on my bed in the dark and began to talk to God out loud.

"Leave me alone," I said with a deep, heavy sigh. "I was fine the way I was, and then You showed up. My life was perfect until You came around. Why'd You have to come along and mess everything up? I don't want to serve You; I made up my mind. I don't believe in You. Unless You can prove to me You are more powerful than the devil I serve, I'm staying in this religion. I'm not going to put my trust in a name. It's just another name to me."

I lay on the bed, about to fall asleep. As my eyes got heavy, my last words came out in a whisper: "If You are more powerful than witchcraft, then show me or leave me alone."

Train Ride to the Abyss

That night God caused me to fall into a deep sleep, and I dreamed. I found myself in a packed subway train, and I knew this train was heading straight to hell. The train was traveling so fast, at a speed I could not imagine. The people's faces looked drained and confused, and I felt as though I could not breathe. I found a spot to grab onto, and there before me was a young woman dressed in a stylish business suit looking into my eyes.

I got a good look at the woman. She had a knockout smile that highlighted a beautiful face. Everything about her was striking. She moved her lips and said something to me. "I'm going to hell, and I'm dragging you with me!" she said in a devilish language.

Fear ripped through me as the young woman reached for my arm. She gripped me with the strength of a man, and when she did I pulled away so hard I jolted myself from sleep. Eyes darting at every corner of my bedroom, I was looking to hide from the attractive pursuer with the demonic voice. But a moment later, I found myself tumbling back into another surreal setting.

This time I stood on a high platform, looking onto the subway tracks below. Beside me was a devil-worshipping cousin of mine. I asked him, "How do I get down from here?"

"If you want to get to the platform, you'll have to slide down that rope." He pointed to a long rope dangling down into the tracks. "Or you can enter the tunnel until you exit onto the street."

The dangling rope looked dangerous, but I wanted to find my way home. So instead I opted for the darkness of the long, foreboding tunnel. The tunnel was narrower than I thought, more pitch black than I imagined. I knew I was not in a normal tunnel but one of the tunnels of hell. How long would I have to be here, strangled in my fear? Walking deeper into the tunnel, I felt uneasy and the fear grew stronger, like no fear I ever felt on earth. Heat emanated from the tunnel, as if I were walking into the mouth of a dragon. With every step I took, my feet sank into a soft, unfamiliar surface. Suddenly, the devil himself stood in front of me. He was over 12 feet tall, with gruesome-looking features and deep red eyes. I noticed that his wings were stained and dirty.

As he spoke, heat came out of his mouth. "I have given you everything: wealth, women, and power," he said in a deep, echoing voice. "People fear you because of me. I was like a father to you, and now you want to throw it all away? Don't you know you can never get rid of me?"

I looked into his churning eyes, and what I saw made me want to run in the direction I had come, but my feet felt cemented to the ground and I couldn't move. I couldn't scream to save my life.

"If you won't serve me," he continued, "then I'll have to destroy you."

He tried to grab me, and I backed up.

"You fool," he said, laughing. "You can't get away. You belong to me!"

As he went to grab me once again, something appeared in my right hand, and I looked at it with amazement. It was a 3-foot cross. As soon as he reached for me, I put the cross on him, and he lost all strength and power and fell to his knees. In shock at what had taken place, I continued running through the tunnel as fast as I could. When I reached the end of the tunnel, the same fear gripped me again, only this time much stronger and much worse. The devil appeared for the second time, angrier than before, speaking to me in demonic tongues and telling me how he was going to destroy me.

"I have no plans of leaving you!" I shouted, my whole body trembling.

He pointed his long finger at me. "You liar!" he said in a screaming voice.

"No, no," I pleaded, "I'm just confused! Bear with me. I'll get it back together."

"No!" he said once again, his voice echoing down the tunnel. "I'm going to keep you here in hell with me so your body on earth won't wake up. You'll be pronounced dead."

When I saw I had no way out, I pulled down my T-shirt and showed him the scars on my chest. "I will use these to destroy you," I said.

He laughed out loud. "You fool. I gave you those scars." The scars were physical evidence of the contract I had made on the night I sold my soul. That infuriated him even more. He attempted to grab me again, this time with a greater fury. As he reached for me, the cross appeared in my right hand for a second time, standing between him and me. I pushed the cross on him, and his strength snapped out of his body and he fell to his knees.

That's when I woke up from my dream. I sat bolt upright in bed, my eyes wide open, my body shaking in a cold sweat. I looked around the room, trying to get my thoughts together. Suddenly I realized it was a dream that God had used to show me He was bigger and more powerful than anything I had served for twenty-five years in witchcraft.

"Oh, my God," I said, my voice shaking. "You *are* real and You do love me. Despite everything I said against You, how I mocked You and laughed at Your church, how I ridiculed Christians, trying to break their faith, and recruited some to the dark side—in spite of all this You still love me. Now, Jesus, I give my life to you. I will serve You instead of the demons, and You will be Lord over my life. You are the true God."

I took out a piece of paper, marking the day in 1999, and wrote out a vow to the Lord that for all the days of my life, I would serve Him and be fully surrendered to His will.

Jesus Christ had delivered me from witchcraft. Never again to return.

Chapter 16

The Real Battle Begins

Filled with a new joy, as I went through the next few days I told many people that I was a born-again Christian. Rachael decided that we should go our separate ways because she wanted to date other people. My life had to go on with Jesus.

One afternoon I was walking down Metropolitan Avenue, coming to the corner of McGraw. A cool fall breeze blew down the sidewalk, and blue skies shone overhead. As I walked along I bumped into an old buddy, Big John. I could see the excitement on his face as I approached him.

"Hey, John, hey John!" he said as we slapped hands. "I have good news for you. I've been wanting to see you, man."

"What's up, Big? What's on your mind?"

"I got this person who's willing to pay you over $10,000 to hire your witchcraft powers. I told them you're the best of the best."

I gave him a broad smile. "Big John, I have better news for you."

He grinned back. "So tell me."

"I'm a born-again Christian now," I said. "I serve Jesus Christ."

Big's face went blank and he went into shock. "No, John, no! You're playing games with me. How could it be? I know you're playing."

"No, I'm not. I'm being truthful with you."

"But it can't be," he said, shaking his head in disbelief.

I glanced over his shoulder. "Hey, here comes my mother," I said as I saw her walking down the sidewalk. "Ask her. She'll tell you."

His voice cracking, Big turned to my mother. "Is it true John is a Christian?"

"Absolutely, yes," my mother said.

Big John stared at me for a moment, saying nothing, and just turned and walked away, crushed by the news that I was no longer the devil worshipper he once knew. Sad to say, in my heart I thought he would be happy for me, but I guess not.

Nighttime Visitations

That night I went home and talked to God before getting ready for bed. It started like any other night. After turning off my bedside lamp, I tucked myself under the covers and fell asleep.

A little after midnight I woke up with a start. *What was it that had awakened me?* Instantly I knew—an evil presence sat next to me on my bed. I braced myself to make sense of what was sitting there. My room had turned ice-cold like a refrigerator, and a heavy presence hung over the room. The presence was so thick I could almost touch it. My stomach knotted, and every hair on my body stood on end.

As I tried to pray, an invisible pair of hands grabbed me by the throat and locked me in a chokehold while I felt I was being lifted off the bed. I gasped for air and tried to fight the thing off me, but I couldn't release myself. Unable to speak, I cried out to Jesus in my thoughts, "Help me, Jesus! Help me, Jesus! Help me!"

Suddenly the hands gripping my throat released me, I dropped back onto the mattress, and everything in the room returned to normal. I barely got any sleep that night, knowing they could come back at any moment.

The next day as I sat at the diner, waiting for my breakfast, I tried to make sense of everything that took place the night before. I opened up my Bible to the book of John and started to read about the life of Jesus to get spiritual strength. "Jesus, I pray that You have control over my life, and help me fight all these evil spirits that I have denounced and left behind to serve You. In Your precious name, amen."

I remembered the many stories I had heard in the occult about those who left the religion or betrayed it and then paid the ultimate price, and I guessed my number had come up. The witches and warlocks of *espiritismo*, Santeria, and Palo wanted me dead. The battle had just begun.

That night as I went to bed, I hoped and prayed that what happened the night before would not repeat itself. Eventually I forced myself to sleep, and in the middle of the night the room went cold again as I became aware of a presence sitting on the opposite side of the bed. That presence decided to lie next to me—I knew I couldn't even turn over because it was so real. The mattress sank down with the weight of the thing lying next to me. Paralyzed with fear, I knew I had to face it, not knowing the outcome of what the night would bring. This went on all night long for many nights in a row.

Other nights, my bed would shake so hard it felt I was being raised off the floor. I wanted to scream aloud in the darkness, but my screams would not come out. The demons that were sent to torment me were trying to separate my body from my spirit. It felt as if they were trying to rip my soul out. Those nights were pure evil. I knew that the demons were sent every night to finish me off. To them I was a traitor, but to Jesus Christ, I became a son. I prayed my heart out for my Savior to rescue me from the dark night of my soul—the anguish and suffering and torment I thought would never stop.

I learned to sleep during the day and pray at night, doing my best to pray, but I didn't know how because I was a baby Christian and had not yet learned to defend myself spiritually against the onslaught of the demons. Insomnia is a terrible thing. Your body begs for sleep, but something from within steals it away—fear! That's what had me awake, night after night, pulse racing, waiting for them to come for me, and come they did.

After thirty days of hell, one night it all came to an end. It left me wondering and asking myself many questions. I asked God repeatedly why He had allowed demon spirits to torment me night after night. He never answered. Sometime later, I got a life-changing response. This time it was God talking. He said, "I wanted to see how much you loved Me."

Burying the Past

As the days moved along, things got brighter and I looked forward to my water baptism—a full immersion the way Jesus had done in the Jordan River. To my surprise I was being accepted by the brothers and sisters in the church, because at one time they did not know how to relate to me because of where I came from. They were either afraid or shy about approaching me. But I thanked God that things were looking up.

"Hey, John, you're being baptized in a few days. How do you feel, man?" Tony said as he greeted me in Bible class.

I smiled. "I feel great and I'm looking forward to it. I'm glad it's coming along and that the Lord Jesus Christ is giving me an opportunity to be baptized."

"Amen to that, John."

A woman named Evelyn turned around and said, "John, we've all been praying for you, and we're so happy you're being baptized."

The warm responses from the people in church touched my heart.

The day leading up to the baptism, we had one final meeting with the pastor. He went over everything that needed to be said and what time we had to be at the church. "The church where you're being baptized is located at Prospect Avenue and 168th Street. Be there on time. The baptism starts at 4:30, so we need you there about four o'clock." I felt a little nervous, with butterflies in my stomach, but the baptism excited me because it was something so different from what I knew for twenty-five years of ceremony after ceremony. This was something that would actually be good for me.

Saturday morning dawned bright, and I jumped out of bed, excited and eager to get to church—so excited I got there at three o'clock in the afternoon. I gathered my belongings in a bag, the extra clothing I would wear after the baptism, and made my way to Prospect Avenue. As I got to the church, the pastors were there along with those who were going to help with the baptism. They separated the men from the women, put us in different rooms, and got us ready for the baptism.

As the service started, I heard the pastor announce to the congregation that a baptism was about to take place. My heart racing at 90 miles an hour, I peeked through a crack in the door of the back room and saw the auditorium filled to capacity with family members and friends gathered there to watch. I breathed a prayer, asking the Holy Spirit to calm my nerves, and then gestured to the other men to go first so I could give myself a chance to calm down.

Finally I looked around the room, and to my amazement I was the only one left there. It was time. As I walked out to the baptism pool in the main auditorium, the entire congregation stood to their feet, cheering and applauding. It was a standing ovation. That day was truly a miracle, that God could take a devil worshipper out of hell and get him baptized in the name of the Father, the Son, and the Holy Spirit. That is truly a miracle—only God can do that.

Chapter 17

'I See Jesus in You'

I was a new creation in Christ. Never again to let anger drive me to get back at people. During one church service I heard a voice say: *Leave the church and return to us. We can forgive and make things right.*

I refused to speak to the demons the way I had done in the past. Instead, I prayed to God in Jesus' name, asking Him to wage war on my behalf. I envisioned a host of heaven's angels surrounding me, giving me the courage to keep pushing myself into the things of God: praying, worshipping, and seeking His face.

Not long after this the Lord released me from Grace and Mercy Fellowship, but I did not return to the devil. Instead I found a wonderful new congregation on Manhattan's west side called Times Square Church. The church was founded in 1987 by David Wilkerson, a pastor whose story became famous worldwide when he preached the gospel of Jesus Christ to gang members in New York City, and most notably one named Nicky Cruz. Nicky's conversion is described in the books *The Cross and the Switchblade* and *Run, Baby, Run*. It was there, at Times Square Church, that I started to settle in, making new friends and signing up for discipleship classes. I was feeling like my old self once more—confident—not intimidated by the sea of faces surrounding me. God's favor was shining down on me like the noonday sun, and eventually the loneliness that gnawed away at me for the longest time lifted.

Facing the Devil on Fifth Avenue

One weekday afternoon, as I was coming across Fifth Avenue at 57th Street, heading to a department store, right there in front of me was this tall, stocky, dark-skinned ex-cult member I hadn't seen in the several years since I became a Christian. He was fourth in rank in the occult. I waited patiently as he crossed the avenue and came up to greet me.

"Hello, John, how are you?" he said, his dark eyes trying to pierce through me. "Long time no see," he added, knowing full well that I was a Christian and to them a traitor.

"I'm doing very well, Will," I said. He stretched out his hand, and as we made contact it felt as if everything on Fifth and 57th went into slow motion. Will refused to let my hand go, and I wondered what was happening as he held it in a firm grip. As he locked eyes with me, unblinking, I broke the grip of the handshake. When it broke, everything went back to normal, at its normal pace. We stood there confronting each other, spiritually, physically, mentally, and emotionally, and he started to shake like he was going into convulsions. I wondered what was going on. Since I hadn't seen him in years, maybe, I thought, he had Parkinson's disease, but I soon realized he was being demon-possessed at two o'clock in the afternoon in the middle of Fifth Avenue. As he tried to speak to me, his eyes rolled back in his head. All I saw were the whites of his eyes. He couldn't control himself and didn't know what was happening, like some force hit him straight on and knocked all his powers away. As Will backed away from me, we said our goodbyes. I continued down the sidewalk, and the Holy Spirit clearly said to me, "He was trying to curse you, and I broke the curse." I praised and thanked my Lord Jesus Christ for loving me and protecting me.

Funeral for a Friend

Several months went by, and one evening I was at my mother's house, when a longtime family friend named Daisy, a *Santera* from years back, showed up for a visit. As we all gathered in the living room, I turned to her and said, "Daisy, how's your life?"

"My life is fine, John," she said. "I'm serving the saints and doing very well."

"Daisy, you're not serving any saints at all, you're serving the devil and his demons in Santeria, and there's no coincidence that I'm here. This is a divine appointment, and Jesus wants to set you free."

Her face went blank for a moment. "John, what are you saying? You were in the religion a lot longer and deeper than I ever will be. You know the saints better than I do—St. Lazarus, St. Ilia, St. Martín, and many others— and you know how this religion works. Why are you speaking about the devil when these saints are supposed to be protective spirits from God, guardian angels that God sent to help us in our daily life?"

I shook my head. "That's not true, that's just a disguise. God doesn't need any help. He's God all by Himself. This religion is the occult, and it's run by the devil and his demons. The reason they use these names is to disguise themselves and entrap people into the religion. Because they know this is the only way you can relate to them. And at one time I was fooled like you are now. Why is it that every feast I went to for twenty-five years, and the feasts you go to, never mentioned Jesus Christ? Isn't that true, Daisy? Have you ever heard them mention Jesus Christ at these gatherings? Have you?"

Daisy stared at me, her eyes troubled. "No, John, not at all."

"So you see," I said, "this is all a masquerade. And another thing, why when you go to the feasts do the people who call themselves mediums get possessed and drink liquor and smoke cigars all night long, and also curse? Where do you see Jesus in this? Jesus Christ is a sovereign God and a holy God."

I could see that in her heart she had a void and couldn't hide it. Her eyes welled up with tears, and she tried to speak but nothing came out.

"Jesus loves you and He died for you," I said softly. "Don't let this opportunity pass you by."

In a very sad voice, she answered, "John, what must I do?"

"Denounce the occult and give your heart to Jesus," I said. "He will set you free."

A few days later, Daisy accepted Jesus as her Lord and Savior, denounced Santeria, and threw all her witchcraft paraphernalia in the trash. I rejoiced to hear the news. But two weeks later I learned that Daisy had passed on to be with the Lord from a cancer that was killing her which she had told no one about. I decided to attend her funeral with a Christian brother who accompanied me.

As we parked in front of the funeral home on Westchester Avenue, I made my way across the street and saw a lady dressed all in white standing guard at the door to the funeral home. Coming closer, I realized she was one of my ex-godmothers in the religion. As I walked by her, she stood stone cold, not even blinking or acknowledging me. I knew what she was up to. I did the same thing for many years. They were there in the funeral home to steal the souls of the dead that were being watched that night.

Inside the front lobby, I saw Aunt Maria and her clan of witches and warlocks. It was more like a reunion, and this time around I was with Jesus. As I turned around and greeted Aunt Maria, her face froze.

She gave me a look that said it all. *"We've been trying to kill you for seven years, and you're still around."*

All I did was smile and make my way to the casket to pay my respects to Daisy. As I came back out to the lobby, many of those in the occult did not look at me or say a word to me. I was their enemy. They looked jittery and uncomfortable, pacing back and forth. I started to pray silently, asking the Holy Spirit what was going on. He said to me, "What does darkness have to do with the light?"

As I said my goodbyes, the Holy Spirit reminded me that I was no longer part of that world. It was like a twenty-five-year nightmare had finally come to an end, and he whom the Son sets free is free indeed. I knew that night, in my heart, that I was truly free.

'I See Jesus in You'

As time went by and I situated myself in the church, I prayed to the Lord and told Him I wanted to be a servant in His house—I wanted to join a ministry. I asked God to direct me to the right opportunity, and as I prayed He led me to join the security ministry at Times Square Church. The Lord had granted me favor there with one of the elders who was in charge of the security team. As I matured spiritually and time went by, I was blessed to be in charge of covering Pastor David Wilkerson, picking him up and walking him home down the city streets after services. I was also assigned to Nicky Cruz and his family whenever he attended Times Square Church to preach. Those were among the many blessings I had, the honor to walk with Pastor Dave and Reverend Nicky and learn from these men of God what He had done in their lives during the many chats I had with them.

One night was like never before—so special. As I walked Pastor Dave home after service that crisp autumn night, I glanced at him. He was an elegant man, thin and fit for his age, well dressed, and I admired the way he took care of himself. I looked up to him like a spiritual dad. But there was something more about this man—he had an anointing on him that was indescribable. As we walked side by side, not saying a word, and approached his home, he turned to me. He could have said many things that night as he looked at me, but the words that came out of his mouth pierced my soul. I've been touched twice in my life—once by Jesus Christ, my Lord and Savior, and the second time by my pastor, as he said words I will never forget: "I see Jesus in you."

I turned my face, my eyes welling up with tears, and I walked away blessed beyond measure. As I headed back up the street toward the church, I recalled as a little boy how I thought God had passed me by. This time He had not passed me by.

There Is a New Life Waiting

In conclusion, I want to make it perfectly clear that the dangers of witchcraft, tarot card reading, the religion, or involvement in any occult are very real. Nothing in the devil's backyard is a game to be toyed with. Although God delivered me, He didn't have to. He didn't owe me anything. He did it simply because of His great love and mercy. Salvation is free but it isn't cheap. It cost the death of His only begotten Son, the shed blood of an innocent man—the Lamb of God who takes away the sin of the world (John 1:29).

As a young man, I tried everything to fill the empty void in my life—booze, women, position, money, and worshipping a god who was really the devil in disguise. But what could truly fill the vastness of the heart? Only God through Jesus Christ can, just as His presence fills the cosmos. He can fill and satisfy your life, just as He did mine. Now I live a life of peace, joy, and unconditional love, knowing that when I die I will be with Him forever.

I have a question for you to think about. If today were your last day on earth, where would you spend eternity? There is no escaping the courtroom of heaven. If you refuse the holy one who bled and died on the cross, the one for whom God poured out His wrath against all sin, the judgment is where you will stand. The Bible says it is appointed unto man to die once, but after that comes the judgment (Hebrews 9:27).

The Sum of All Things

King Solomon said in the book of Ecclesiastes:

Now all has been heard; here is the conclusion of the matter: Fear God and keep his com-mandments, for this is the whole [duty] of man. For God will bring every deed into judg-ment, including every hidden thing, whether it is good or evil.
Ecclesiastes 12:13-14 NIV

Today looking back at my life, I realize like King Solomon that all was meaninglessness. Witchcraft added nothing to my life; it destroyed my marriage and stole my relationship with my daughter in her younger years. It filled my life with misery. It turned me into a man of hatred, pride, and loneliness—a man with a shallow life. It was I who was held captive more than those I cursed. I thought I had it all but in reality I was empty. Empty of true life! Jesus said in John 10:10, "*I am come that they might have life, and that they might have it more abundantly.*"

How grateful I am to have true life today. It has not always been an easy walk. Like everyone else my life is not void of sorrows or disappointments, even in Jesus. But I have something now that outweighs any day in my previous life, and that is the unconditional love of God. I have been set free and there is no greater miracle than the miracle of the salvation of my soul.

I don't know if your soul is imprisoned by the religion or any other occult. Perhaps certain areas of your life have not yet experienced true freedom. There is a God with open arms who wants to set you totally free. If He could take a sinner like me who cursed His name, a man who knew nothing but darkness and bring him to the light, then there is hope and a future for you today. I cannot close the story of my life without offering you the precious gift that was so freely given to me when I was bound and could not see my way out of darkness. This gift is Jesus.

Pray this prayer with me:

Lord, I thank You for the transforming power that comes through Your Son, Jesus. I too want to experience true freedom and abundant life. I repent today of all my sins. I repent if at any time in my life I opened myself to the occult. I ask You to come into my life now and be Lord and Savior over my life. Wash me with Your blood, which is ever flowing, and transform my life forever. In Jesus' name. Amen.

I declare now over your life that every chain of Satan is broken, that the blood of Jesus shed on the cross is washing and cleansing every area of your being. Today I declare freedom in Christ Jesus over you. Amen.

John Ramirez

To My Dad

No doubt, my dad and I were never able to establish the son and father relationship that should have been. But I have forgiven my dad. Healing could never have taken place in my life without forgiveness.

I thank God for changing my heart and bringing His healing balm to the broken pieces of my life. In a time when even thinking of those who hurt me would literally take my breath away, I discovered the unconditional love of God which surpasses all pain and understanding. He taught me the true meaning of forgiveness.

Forgiveness is a choice. When I look at how Christ forgave those who hurt Him while hanging on the cross, it melts my heart. So I chose to forgive. I realize today that I love my dad. Good or bad, he was still my father. I wonder, if he were still alive, how things would have been different. Perhaps I will see my dad again. Although he was not saved, I do not know if in his last breaths he cried out for God's forgiveness. The criminal on the cross next to Jesus found Paradise through his last-minute repentance.

I know this: I was a blasphemer and a mocker and somehow Jesus stretched out His hand to me. So one day I will know if God in His everlasting mercy stretched out His love to my father. *"For His ways are higher than our ways."* Praise be to God.

I love you, Dad, and I miss you. Thank You, Lord, for depositing in me one of your greatest gifts—the gift of forgiveness.

—John

Unmasking Santeria

Santeria is a Spanish term that roughly translated means "worship of saints." The Bible states that *"my people perish for lack of knowledge."* Therefore, I am compelled to bring you to all truth by exposing and revealing insight into the history of Santeria (also linked to *espiritismo* and Palo Mayombe)—a religion that outwardly professes to be good, but in reality is witchcraft. Between the mid-1600s and 1800s, over twelve million Africans were forced out of the land they loved, brought across the vast Atlantic, and forced into an inhumane life of slavery, freed only by death, then carried on by succeeding generations. They took nothing with them except the clothing they wore on their backs and a tradition of religion that was a way of life for them—a religion of voodoo.

Many of the West African slaves endured a three-month journey to Cuba. These slaves had two things in common: their oppressors and voodoo. To maintain rule, the slave masters came up with a plan to enforce a new belief system for the slaves, knowing that these slaves possessed great power through the use of voodoo magic. Roman Catholicism would now replace the beliefs that native Africans had brought with them. But the slaves were clever people. They came up with a way to remain true to the religion of their homeland by disguising voodoo idols as Catholic saints. The devotees of *espiritismo*, Santeria, and Palo Mayombe are no different from the slaves who were entrapped by this religion.

African slaves used other Roman Catholic saints to cover up this evil practice. Through this dark practice of worship, slaves kept "the religion" alive by the trickeries of Satan. Now, centuries later, this same voodoo practice has changed its appearance once more, adapting itself to this generation and culture and the lifestyles that people live today. It has gone mainstream. No Catholic priest would ever send you to *centros* (spiritualism churches) or to a fortuneteller. This religion continues to disguise itself through saints in the practices of *espiritismo*, Santeria, and Palo Mayombe, and will continue to change in order to grow in strength and perpetuate its beliefs. Satan is a master of disguise and has no intentions of retiring. What he has done to millions in the past he continues to do today. His objective is clear: to spiritually blind as many people as possible, thus keeping them from entering the glorious kingdom of God and His Son Jesus Christ.

The Lies of the Enemy

The religion involves people known as mediums. Mediums are those who lend their bodies to demonic spirits in order to speak and perform works through a physical body. I was one of those people! This religion uses many tools to keep people from coming into a relationship with Jesus Christ. The devil and his demons use things that the human race can easily relate to, for example, giving themselves names, birthdays, places where they were born, and families they once had. This is done so that people can find something to relate to—it is called "common ground." This is a lie, for the spirits that mediums channel are fallen angels without identity.

How you are fallen from heaven, O Lucifer, son of the morning! How you are cut down to the ground, You who weakened the nations! For you have said in your heart: 'I will ascend into heaven, I will exalt my throne above the stars of God; I will also sit on the mount of the congregation on the farthest sides of the north; I will ascend above the heights of the clouds, I will be like the Most High. Yet you shall be brought down to Sheol, to the lowest depths of the Pit.   Isaiah 14:12-15

The devil and his demons will never speak the truth because the Bible says the devil is the father of lies (John 8:44) and has been lying from the beginning. But let's just say they were to tell the truth about who they really are. Would you really want to be in that religion called *espiritismo*, Santeria, or Palo Mayombe? If you were to meet someone who told you he murdered people for a living, would you want to be in a relationship with that person? This is the same as being involved in this religion because the devil and his demons are murderers. They not only murder your spirit but are assigned to take lives and destroy whatever they are assigned to. They are spiritual hit men.

The devil and his demons adopt names in Santeria like *Obatala*, *Yemaya*, *Ochun*, and *Elegua* to identify themselves with the people they want to entrap. They also use other names to adopt the other aspects of the religion, which are *espiritismo* and Palo Mayombe. But they are all the same demons operating in the spirit realm with three different names trying to copy the sovereignty of God in the trinity: the Father, the Son, and the Holy Spirit. They even create books that have crosses on the front cover as well as the face of Jesus to trick you into believing that this religion is connected to Jesus.

Every book that pertains to this religion never mentions anything about the virgin birth or Jesus being crucified for the sins of the world. They make no mention of the Lord's resurrection, His second coming, or His being Savior of the world.

Botanicas—the Dark Side

Many people are in the habit of visiting *botanicas*, or potion stores, thinking they are making innocent purchases of so-called white magic and statues such as *La Madama*, Francisco and Francisca, *San Lazaro, Santa Barbara, Siete Potencias, indios*, and *congos*. The Lord said in the first commandment, in Exodus 20:3-6*:*

> *Thou shall have no other gods before me. Thou shall not make for yourself any graven image, or any likeness of anything that is in heaven above or that is in the earth beneath, or that is in the water under the earth. Thou shall not bow down to them nor serve them, for I thy God am a jealous God, visiting the iniquity of the fathers upon the children unto the third and fourth generation of them that hate me, but showing mercy unto thousands of them that love me and keep my commandments.*

Espiritismo is a religious movement about money, pride, greed, envy, and attaining status. It made boasters out of all of us, and because of that we had no respect for anyone, nor did we fear God. Every year on Holy Week, we would discredit God by mocking what the Bible taught. Through animal sacrifices and the casting of spells, we destroyed people's lives whenever we felt like it. And it was all done without any guilt or conscience—all in the name of God.

This is the way the devil has deceived mankind. From generation to generation he has kept men from having a true relationship with Jesus Christ. People have become victims of the enemy's plans and his lies. Praise be to God, He has a plan and a way out for all through His Son, Jesus Christ.

> *For God so loved the world that He gave His only begotten Son, that whoever believes in Him should not perish but have everlasting life.* John 3:16

A Testimony of God's Amazing Grace

I was not sure if I wanted to add this story as part of my testimony in this book. After I heard from the Holy Spirit, who spoke to my heart, I knew God wanted the world to know, both believers and unbelievers—especially those who are struggling or have strayed—about His amazing grace.

I remember one day in my devil-worshipping days God brought to remembrance a couple that I knew who were also involved in the religion. They were married for many years. One day the husband fell in love with another woman at his workplace. This affair went on for a very long time. His wife, Maria, started to notice changes going on in her marriage by her husband's behavior. Sometime later she started to follow her husband when he would leave the house. One day she confronted him while he was making a call from a pay phone on the street to the other woman. A big scandal took place in the family to the point that she was thinking of divorcing her husband. But she thought of a better idea. "Why let this woman keep my husband

and I lose everything? Instead, I can hire John Ramirez to kill her through witchcraft and still keep my husband."

Sometime later I got a phone call from Maria, crying and telling me everything that had happened between her and her husband, how he had been unfaithful, and that she would give me anything I wanted if I would cast a spell and kill this other woman through witchcraft. My response was to give me a few days and I would think about it. I went behind the scenes and called out the devil to ask permission to destroy the other woman, and his answer was yes. He would give me all the power I needed to accomplish her death, and he gave me a recipe from the pit of hell on how to get it done.

Days later Maria stopped by and asked me how much it would cost for me to kill this woman with witchcraft. I told her $10,000, but something strange happened as Maria was walking out of my apartment. She turned to me and said, "By the way, this woman is a Christian." I stopped Maria in her tracks and said, "If that's the case, it will be my pleasure to do it for free. I hate these fake church-going people, and I'm going to teach her the lesson of a lifetime." Even though I worshipped the devil, I knew of God and His ways. But I also knew that He was my enemy. So I was determined to destroy this so-called Christian woman. The spell was cast. Because I also had a relationship with Maria's husband, I waited and hoped that someday he would inform me that his mistress was on her deathbed. He did not have a clue that I had a mandate from the devil to take her out.

As months went by there was no news reported about her condition. So I started one night to call on the demons assigned to kill her, but there was no response. All

I knew was that she was still going to church from time to time even though she was involved with a married man. One night while at home, I heard the voice of the devil telling me that his mission of killing her had been aborted. I was so angry I kept asking why. "Why do we have to stop now?" I asked. "It's just a matter of days and she will be dead. I don't want to stop. Kill her. My reputation is on the line. She must die." The devil, with a loud voice, said, "No! Her God said leave her alone."

I was in awe of the whole thing. Even though she was committing adultery, through God's amazing grace and the love of Jesus Christ, God had mercy on her. There was no devil in hell, in *espiritismo,* and in Palo Mayombe that could take her life because God had placed a hedge of protection around her. That was true love. Now that I am saved, I understand how incredible God's love is, even for the backslider. There are many stories in the Old Testament such as the life of David, who committed adultery and murder, yet God had mercy on him. Or Moses, who committed murder, but God had mercy on him as well. In the New Testament we hear of a woman who was caught in the very act of adultery. Though many wanted to stone her, again Jesus had mercy on her. There is no other love or grace in the universe bigger than the love of Jesus. *"And now abide faith, hope, love, these three; but the greatest of these is love"* (1 Corinthians 13:13).

Pila's Testimony: I wanted to share this with all of you. I just reconnected with a brother in Christ, John, after many years. I first met him after he had gotten saved in 1999, when another sister in Christ and I went to meet him. We didn't even know him but heard a little bit of his testimony and wanted to hear more for ourselves. So we met up with him at some pizza joint on the Upper East Side near where he lives. I have to say that I was completely riveted by his testimony of the life he left behind in Palo Mayombe, which is the deadliest, darkest side of the religion. He basically was serving Satan. However, he came to the Lord, which is a miracle in and of itself. To my knowledge, study, and experience, no one gets out of this life alive. It's obvious that God's hand was upon him.

I had the privilege of meeting John in his humble beginnings. I actually had the heart and desire to encourage him as I remember telling him that God was going to use him in a mighty way and that he would one day write a book. Well, I'm happy to report that his first book is now out. To God be ALL the glory! Hallelujah! Praise His holy name!

Lucy's Testimony: My name is Lucy. I lived in Parkchester in the Bronx for eleven years. One summer day my daughter, Monique, and I decided to go for a walk. She was expecting her third child.

As we were walking down Metropolitan Avenue, a man dressed in white from head to toe walked by. We noticed he had a cross around his neck that was hanging upside down. My daughter said, "I'm crossing the street, I don't want to walk by that evil man." I was young in the Lord but I said, "In the name of Jesus, how could anyone have a cross hanging upside down?" Every hair on my body stood up. I immediately started to plead the blood of Jesus over myself and on this man dressed in white.

Throughout those years, as I waited for the bus, I would see this mysterious man dressed in white. Every time I saw him I would pray for him, praying that one day he would come out of darkness and into the light.

In September 2006, I moved to Orlando, Florida. It is here that I found a church where I started learning more and growing in my relationship with the Lord. One day, I met this mysterious man (John Ramirez) as he and his friend drove from New York looking for the pastor of the Orlando church. As I saw John, he did not have the evil look as he did in New York. He informed me that he was no longer serving the enemy but was serving the Lord wholeheartedly.

I was really excited for John. Seeing how the Lord could change his life in such an awesome way, I began to praise my Lord, thanking Him for the transformation of John's body, mind, and spirit. I give God all the glory and praise.

Norma's Testimony: My name is Norma, and this is how I came to know John Ramirez. Back in the early '90s, my sister in the Lord and I routinely met every week at a neighborhood diner on Parkchester Avenue in the Bronx. I used to see this young man, always dressed in white from head to toe, and I knew by his attire that he was *Santero*. His appearance impressed me. He was a tall, handsome young man with jet-black hair, olive skin, and dark eyes. He seemed to be intelligent. Yet he was involved in such an evil lifestyle. The first thing that came out of me was: "Lord, deliver him from this evil life!" There was an aching feeling in my heart for him, although I didn't know him, but God did, and this was sufficient, for only He could put this burden or care in our hearts for a stranger, and the Word says we must pray for lost souls (2 Pet. 3:9). Every time I'd see him, when walking or standing at the bus stop, he would pass by me and I'd get chills and a kind of fear would take hold of me, but immediately I would plead the blood of Christ over me and against those evil spirits that had this young man bound.

One day as my friend and I were meeting at the diner, he (John) walked in, and right away I started praying and extended my hand in his direction. My friend got afraid and said to stop and that besides people were staring at me. My answer was: "I couldn't care less about it, for this is more important. My concern is for the strongholds in his life to be broken and for him to see the light of Christ and have that encounter with Jesus." As I prayed, all of a sudden he turned around looking in our direction as if someone or something got his attention. Quickly I put my hand down, but I finished my prayer. For a couple of years after that day, I didn't see him. I thought he'd probably moved away. Nonetheless I prayed he would get saved and delivered.

Lo and behold, my daughter's best friend had invited me to visit her church, and one Sunday I decided to go and asked my sister and a very dear friend to come with me. We went to the address and couldn't find it, for there was only this old house and no sign or church name to identify it. We walked back and forth, and I walked a little behind them, when all of a sudden I heard someone asking what we were looking for and if he could help. My sister told him we were looking for the church, and he said: "You're right here. Come, follow me." But I froze and didn't move. *My God, this is the young man from Parkchester! The voodoo guy. This is a setup from Satan. This might be a Santeria place.* They were calling me and I was scared, but they followed him inside. I walked behind in case I had to run. Then I saw Ellie, my daughter's friend, and my senses came back to me.

As I came into the church and sat down, I told the person who invited me, "He used to be the witchcraft guy. Now he's saved? There were several times that I prayed for him as he passed me by. It felt like hell had passed me by." Ellie insisted that I tell him, but I said no, it is sufficient that the Lord knows, but she told him. John came and thanked me for my prayers and of course wanted to hear all the details.

I thank God for John's salvation and deliverance!

Certificate of Legal Blindness

New York State Office of Children and Family Services
Commission for the Blind and Visually Handicapped
Capital View Office Park
South Building, Room 201
52 Washington Street
Rensselaer, NY 12144-2796

Verification of Legal Blindness

Name:	CBVH Registration No.
John Ramirez	CF# D5707Q

The above named person is registered as legally blind with the Commission for the Blind and Visually Handicapped in accordance with New York State law, Section 8704.

Signature: *Kenneth Gilerman*
Title: Director, Program Evaluation and Support
Date: 10/05/2009

This is an image of the New York State Office of Family Services Commission for the Blind and Visually Handicapped, confirming that I was legally blind.

Things That God Hates

Mediums

Leviticus 20:27—A man also or a woman that has a familiar spirit, or that is a wizard, shall surely be put to death.

Leviticus 19:31—Regard not them that have familiar spirits, neither seek after wizards to be defiled by them. I am the Lord your God.

Witchcraft

Micah 5:12—And I will cut off witchcrafts out of your hand, and you shall have no more soothsayers.

1 Samuel 15:23—Rebellion is as the sin of witchcraft.

Galatians 5:20-21—The deeds of the flesh are... the worship of idols, witchcraft...those that practice such things shall not inherit the kingdom of God.

Magic

Acts 19:19—And many of them which used curious arts, brought their books together and burned them before all men.

Revelation 21:8—But the fearful, and unbelieving, and the abominable...and sorcerers [magicians, wizards]...shall have their part in the lake that burns with fire and brimstone.

Acts 8:9-13—A certain man named Simon, bewitched the people of Samaria with sorceries [magic], to whom they all gave heed. But when they believed Philip's preaching...the kingdom of God and the name of Jesus Christ, they were baptized [repented and turned away from sorcery].

Isaiah 57:3-4—You sons of sorceresses. Are you not children of rebellion, offspring of deceit?

Jeremiah 27:9—Hearken not to your sorcerers.

Revelation 22:15—Outside [the gates of the city of heaven] are the sorcerers...and anyone who loves and practices lying.

Speaking to the Dead
Deuteronomy 18:10-11—There shall not be found among you any one that...consults familiar spirits, or a wizard, or a necromancer [one who conjures up the dead].

Wicked Sacrifices
Psalm 106:36-37—And they served their idols which were a snare unto them. Yea, they sacrificed their sons and their daughters unto devils.

Idols

Psalm 115:4-8—Their idols are silver and gold, the work of men's hands. They have mouths, but they do not speak; eyes they have, but they do not see; they have ears, but they do not hear; noses they have, but they do not smell; they have hands, but they do not handle; feet they have, but they do not walk, nor do they mutter through their throat. Those who make them are like them. So is everyone who trusts in them.

Isaiah 2:8, 18—Their land also is full of idols... and the idols he [God] shall utterly abolish [destroy].

Deuteronomy 12: 3—Tear down their altars and smash their sacred stone pillars...chop down their idols so that they will never again be worshipped.

Judges 2:17—But the Israelites paid no attention to their leaders. Israel was unfaithful to the Lord and worshipped other gods.

Ezekiel 6:13—Then shall you know that I am the Lord, when their slain men shall be among their idols.

1 John 5:21—My children, keep yourselves from idols.

Jeremiah 2:8—My priests did not know me, rulers rebelled against me. The prophets spoke in the name of Baal and worshipped useless idols.

Astrology

Isaiah 47:11,13—Therefore evil shall come upon you....Let now the astrologers, the stargazers, the monthly prognosticators, stand up and save you from these things that shall come upon you [God's wrath].

Familiar Spirits

Isaiah 29:4—Thou shall be brought down [God's judgment], and shall speak out of the ground, and your speech shall be low out of the dust as of one that has a familiar spirit.

1 Samuel 28:9—Thou knowest what Saul has done, how he has cut off [killed] those that have familiar spirits.

Isaiah 8:19-20—When men tell you to consult mediums and spiritists, who whisper and mutter, should not a people inquire of their God? Why consult the dead on behalf of the living?...If they do not speak according to this word, they have no light of dawn.

Devil Worship

Matthew 4:9-10—"All this will I give you," the devil said [to Jesus]. "If you fall down and worship me." Then Jesus said, "Be gone, Satan, for it is written: worship the Lord thy God and serve him only."

This is how the religion entraps you—by using tactics to make you believe those who practice it (mediums, spiritualists, fortunetellers) are a part of Jesus Christ and His kingdom. These are some of the many tools the devil and his demons use.

Need additional copies?

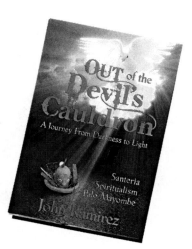

To order more copies of
Out of the Devil's Cauldron,
contact JohnRamirez.org

Also available at:
Amazon.com
Barnesandnoble.com

Call 917-587-1127 for multiple copy discounts!

To invite John Ramirez to speak at your conference/event
or for TV or radio inquiries and any additional information,
please contact John Ramirez Ministries at:
917-587-1127
or reach him at JohnRamirez.org

a division of John Ramirez Ministries

CPSIA information can be obtained
at www.ICGtesting.com
Printed in the USA
FFOW01n0159120318
45625001-46437FF